Pure Faith

Book of Prayer

Pure Faith

BOOK OF PRAYER

Jason Evert

Totus Tuus
PRESS

Denver

2013

Published by Totus Tuus Press
PO Box 280021, Lakewood, CO 80228
www.totustuuspress.com

NIHIL OBSTAT: I have concluded that the materials presented in this work are
free of doctrinal and moral errors.
Bernadeane M. Carr, SLT, March 27, 2007

IMPRIMATUR: In accord with 1983 CIC 827 § 3,
permission to publish this work is hereby granted.
Robert H. Brom, Bishop of San Diego, March 28, 2007

Cover design by Devin Schadt   Interior design by Claudine Mansour Design
Printed in the United States of America
ISBN Hardcover: 978-0-9830923-4-6   Paperback: 978-0-9913754-7-9

Make up your mind to become a saint.

St. Mary Mazzarello

You cannot be half a saint. You must be a whole saint or no saint at all.

St. Therese of Lisieux

In order to be a saint, you have to seriously want to be one.

Bl. Teresa of Calcutta (Mother Teresa)

Dear young people, have the sacred ambition to become holy like he is holy! You will ask me: but is it possible today to be saints? If we had to rely only on human strength, the undertaking would be truly impossible. With Christ, saintliness—the divine plan for every baptized person—becomes possible. . . . Young people of every continent, do not be afraid to be the saints of the new millennium!

Pope John Paul II

Contents

How to Pray   I

Morning Prayers   17

Prayers to the Holy Spirit   23

Prayers to Mary   27

Prayers to Saints   45

Prayers for Confession   63

Prayers for Mass   79

Prayers before the Blessed Sacrament   89

Chaplet of Divine Mercy   99

Stations of the Cross   103

Prayers for Specific Intentions   105

Evening Prayers   163

Appendix: Recommended Reading   171

Pure Faith
Book of Prayer

how to Pray

Bl. Teresa of Calcutta (Mother Teresa):
I worry some of you still have not really met Jesus—one to one—you and Jesus alone. We may spend time in chapel, but have you seen with the eyes of your soul how he looks at you with love? Do you really know the living Jesus, not from books but from being with him in your heart? Have you heard the loving words he speaks to you? Ask for the grace: He is longing to give it.

Until you can hear Jesus in the silence of your own heart, you will not be able to hear him saying

"I thirst" in the hearts of the poor. Never give up this daily intimate contact with Jesus as the real living person—not just the idea. How can we last even one day without hearing Jesus say "I love you"? Impossible. Our soul needs that as much as the body needs to breathe the air. If not, prayer is dead—meditation, only thinking. Jesus wants you each to hear him speaking in the silence of your heart.

Be careful of all that can block that personal contact with the living Jesus. The devil may try to use the hurts of life—and sometimes our own mistakes—to make you feel it is impossible that Jesus really loves you, is really cleaving to you. This is a danger for all of us. And so sad, because it is completely the opposite of what Jesus is really wanting, waiting to tell you. Not only that he loves you, but even more—he longs for you. He misses you when you don't come close. He thirsts for you. He loves you always, even when you don't feel worthy. When not accepted by others, even by yourself sometimes, he is the one who always accepts you. Only believe—you are precious to him. Bring all you are suffering to his feet—only open your heart to be loved by him as you are. He will do the rest.

———

The prayers collected in this book are holy words. But they're only the start of devotion. As Mother Teresa said, in order for your prayer life to deepen, you must go beyond the written words of others to the unspoken words in your heart.

Prayer is a conversation of love where you speak from the heart and listen patiently. St. Teresa of Avila says, "Mental prayer in my opinion is nothing else than an intimate sharing between friends: It means taking time frequently to be alone with him whom we know loves us."

Imagine having a friend who constantly talked to you but refused to listen. Obviously, you'd never end up becoming very close to this person, because he never made the effort to get to know you. The same goes with prayer: Even if you talk to God constantly, your relationship with him will not deepen until you learn to listen to him. St. John Vianney suggests, "When it's God who is speaking . . . the proper way to behave is to imitate someone who has an irresistible curiosity and who listens at keyholes. You must listen to everything God says at the keyhole of your heart."

Mother Teresa maintained that "the first requirement for prayer is silence. People of prayer are people of silence." When she was asked by an American reporter, "What do you say to God when you pray?" she replied, "Nothing. I just listen." Intrigued by her reply, he continued, "And what does God say to you?" "Nothing," said Mother Teresa. "God just listens."

It's reasonable to wonder what they're listening to if neither one is talking. But for two people deeply in love, words aren't necessary. A man who understood this well was Pope John Paul II, who recommended to young people that if they want to encounter Christ, "above all, create silence in your interior. Let that ardent desire to see God arise from the depth of your hearts, a desire that at times is suffocated by the noise of the world and the seduction of pleasures."

One reason many people struggle in prayer is that they wake up to music, watch television over breakfast, listen to the radio in the car, talk all day, and then go home to the Internet, the phone, and more television. None of these things are bad, but if people could just turn off some of the noise, they would find it easier to be still in prayer.

Imagine a glass of water being stirred into a whirlpool. That's like the busyness of minds throughout the day. If you were to take that glass and suddenly place it on something still, the water would continue to swirl for some time before it was peaceful. The same goes for minds when people stop to pray. If you rush in and out of prayer, you shouldn't be surprised if you don't get much out of the experience. That's why Psalm 37:7 advises that people should "be still before the Lord, and wait patiently for him." When you begin to make room for silence throughout the day, prayer will come more naturally and frequently. Then, when you speak to the Lord, take the advice of these three saints to heart:

> How can you ask to be heard by God when you yourself aren't even paying attention to what you say?
>
> *St. Cyprian of Carthage*

Anyone who has the habit of speaking before God's majesty as if he were speaking to a slave, careless about how he is speaking, and saying whatever comes into his head and whatever he's learned from saying prayers at other times, in my opinion, is not praying. Please, God, may no Christian pray in this way.

St. Teresa of Avila

If someone, simply as an experiment, should try with determination to make his mind touch on as many and as diverse objects as possible, I hardly think that in so short a time he could run through such diverse and numerous topics as the mind, unrestrained, wanders through while the mouth negligently mutters through the most common prayers.

St. Thomas More

Prayer is a battle with distractions that are bound to come, so don't get upset by them. Move forward, because only when you realize that you don't know how to pray is God able to teach you. If you often find yourself rambling on, consider the advice of Mother Teresa:

If you pray with words, let them be filled with love and come from the depths of your heart. Pray with great respect and trust. Fold your hands, close your eyes and lift up your heart to the Lord. Let your prayer be a pure sacrifice to God. Do not pray loud and not too quiet. Pray simply. Let your heart speak. Praise the Lord with all your soul. Words will come like that from the bottom of your heart and you will find joy in prayer. Stop once in a while by a word and think it over, let it sink to the bottom of your heart. Keep them during the rest of the day: They will bring you peace.

So, where do you begin? To learn to pray, make time for prayer. In Mark 1:35, it says that Jesus rose very early before dawn and went off to a deserted place, where he prayed. Learn from this that Jesus set aside a time and place to be alone and free from distractions.

When a couple begins to fall in love, they look forward to the times they'll run into each other. As their commitment deepens, they'll schedule time to see each other. And to the extent that they love each other, they'll make time for one another, no matter how busy life becomes. It's the same with prayer. You may have "run into" God at a retreat, but for the relationship to deepen, you must make time for it. If you pray only when you feel like it, your spiritual life will become selfish. You'll pray because you want something, not because your soul needs it and God deserves it. Then, your life will reflect that same mentality, where you follow God only when you feel like it.

So, tonight—and every night—set your alarm clock ten minutes early. When you arise, you will have ten extra minutes—before you speak to anyone else—to speak with Christ. Eventually, you may want to bump it up to fifteen or thirty minutes, but five or ten minutes is a good place to start. Consistency in simple prayers is far better than saying huge prayers irregularly.

During this morning prayer time, you could thank God for the gift of life, pray the morning prayers in this book, or talk to him about your upcoming day. Consider how you might serve the Lord throughout the day, and think of where, when, and how you are most likely to fall away from him. For example, if you are likely to be sarcastic to a family member or tempted by lust at a certain time, consider how you will avoid those sins and ask for God's grace to overcome them. Then, if you encounter a situation where you're temped, you will have prepared yourself though prayer to meet that challenge. Give your day and your life to God immediately upon rising so that you may enter your day with the spirit of Christ.

Throughout the day, any of the prayers in this book are good to offer. But anything as simple as "Jesus, I trust in you," "Come, Holy Spirit," or saying the name "Jesus" is a great way to love God. One ancient and simple prayer known as the Jesus Prayer is "Lord Jesus Christ, Son of God, have mercy on me, a sinner."

But you don't even need to use words. You could simply smile at God as a prayer. As Mother Teresa said:

My secret is quite simple—I pray! . . . You can pray while you work. Work doesn't stop prayer, and prayer doesn't stop work. It requires only that small raising of the mind to him: I love you, God,

I trust you, I believe in you, I need you now. Small things like that. They are wonderful prayers. Keep close to Jesus. He loves you.

She added:

Love to pray. Feel often during the day the need for prayer, and take the trouble to pray. Prayer enlarges the heart until it is capable of containing God's gift of himself. Ask and seek and your heart will grow big enough to receive him and keep him as your own.

If you don't know what to say in prayer, consider the five kinds of prayer: adoration, petition, intercession, thanksgiving, and praise.

Adoration is blessing and giving honor to God, often in respectful silence.

In petition, you ask the Lord for whatever you need: forgiveness, courage, hope, guidance, etc.

In intercession, you lift up the needs of others: the sick, those who are lonely, family members, enemies, etc.

In thanksgiving, you bless God for everything in

life, the joys as well as the crosses. By doing so, you
follow the instruction of Paul, who wrote, "Give
thanks in all circumstances; for this is the will of
God in Christ Jesus for you" (1 Thess. 5:18).

Praise is when you worship God not so much
for what he does but because of who he is.

Here's another helpful way to focus during your
prayer time: Remember the acronym A.R.R.R.
First, invite the Holy Spirit to help you to pray.
Then, *acknowledge* what's stirring within your heart
at that hour. What are you feeling? Are you joyful, anxious, afraid, or confused? Allow yourself
to feel these emotions. Then, *relate* them to Jesus.
Slowly go through each one, and share them with
him. Third, *receive* his guidance and consolation. To
do this, create silence in your soul and give him
the opportunity to speak to you. Finally, *respond*
to these graces. Make a resolution for how you
will act upon what you received in prayer. If you
don't feel that you're receiving much in prayer, do
not worry. The fruit of prayer is often not experienced during prayer. As one saint said, "Persevere
in prayer. Persevere, even when your efforts seem
barren. Prayer is always fruitful." There's no need

to doubt God's loving presence in our lives if our prayer feels dry. Pope Francis assured us, "We all have in our hearts some areas of unbelief. Let us say to the Lord: I believe! Help my unbelief."

If you don't know when to pray, remember the words of Paul, who tells us in I Thessalonians 5:17, "Pray constantly." This doesn't mean that you should live in a church but rather that all of your life—your studies, your sports, your sufferings, even your dates—are offered as if they were prayers. *Everything* you do should become a prayer. If not, then it isn't worth doing. St. John Bosco reported:

> A saint was once asked, while playing happily with his companions, what he would do if an angel told him that in a quarter of an hour he would die and have to appear before the judgment seat of God. The saint promptly replied that he would continue playing because he was certain these games were pleasing to God.

Besides offering all of your activities as a prayer, if you are able to go to daily Mass, this does your soul more good than you will ever know. You'll also receive many spiritual insights from reading the Bible and the lives of the saints. Lastly, a daily rosary takes only about fifteen minutes, and the full twenty decades less than an hour. If you don't feel ready for a daily rosary, that's okay. Start with one Hail Mary a day. Whatever you are ready for, be generous with God, and he will be more than generous with you. If you're not sure where to pray, try spending time alone in your own room or before the Blessed Sacrament in a church.

For evening prayer, the prayers included in this book are a good place to begin. With them, make a simple examination of conscience. To do this, thank God for giving you this day, and consider how you spent it. Every one of us will render an account to God for every word we speak and every moment we spend, so it's a good idea to begin checking ourselves now. Think about where you have spent your time, who you have spent it with, and how you have acted and thought. If you have difficulty with this, break the day into smaller parts, and consider each part of the day. Ask forgiveness for your sins and thank God for the good that you have done. Say a few prayers for friends, family, and even enemies. Perhaps you can choose a very specific intention, such as the woman who will go to bed tonight afraid and alone, planning an abortion in the morning.

God relies on our prayers to aid in the conversion of others, so it's a beautiful thing to fall asleep while praying for souls. St. Francis de Sales counsels to "never omit this exercise [evening prayer] any more than that of the morning, for as by the latter you open the windows of your soul to the sun of righteousness, so by these evening devotions you close them against the darkness of hell." Other than these daily devotions, make sure, at the least, to attend Mass on Sundays and holy days, and try to go to confession at least monthly. This forms a spiritual plan of life that will keep you united to Christ.

As your prayer life deepens, do not be surprised or discouraged if your time with God seems dry and dull. Such times in prayer are very pleasing to God because it shows that you're trying to grow in faith without having to rely on spiritual pleasures. The world expects instant gratification, a mindset that often slips into spiritual lives. When your meditations are not filled with consolations, insights, and constant joy, you can begin to wonder if you're really praying at all. This can lead to impatience and discouragement, causing you to trouble yourself by trying to feel something. It is then that you must realize that spiritual feelings are not the measure of spiritual growth.

Whether you receive much in prayer or little, accept it. In the words of St. Francis de Sales:

> He who truly loves prayer loves it for the love of God, and he who loves it for the love of God wishes to experience in it nothing but what God is pleased to send him.
>
> You tell me that you cannot pray well. But what better prayer could there be than to represent to God again and again, as you are doing, your nothingness and misery? The most touching appeal that beggars can make is to merely expose to us their deformities and necessities. But there are times when you cannot even do this much, you say, and that you remain there like a statue. Well, even that is better than nothing. Kings and

princes have statues in their palaces for no other purpose than they may take pleasure in looking at them: Be satisfied then to fulfill the same office in the presence of God, and when it so pleases him he will animate the statue.

One saint said that the world is going through a crisis because people do not pray, or they pray little and badly. So, become men and women of prayer. Do not give up in this pursuit of God, but have the attitude of St. John Bosco, who said, "First tell the devil to rest, and then I'll rest, too."

Jason Evert

Morning Prayers

An apostle who does not pray regularly and methodically will necessarily fall into lukewarmness . . . and he will then cease to be an apostle.

St. Josemaria Escriva

When I awake, let me be filled with your presence.

Ps. 17:15 (NAB)

Prayers

Morning Offering

O Jesus, through the Immaculate Heart of Mary I offer you my prayers, works, joys, and sufferings of this day in union with the holy sacrifice of the Mass throughout the world. I offer them for all the intentions of your Sacred Heart: for the salvation of souls, reparation for sin, the reunion of all Christians. I offer them for all the intentions of our bishops and all apostles of prayer and in particular for those recommended by our Holy Father this month. Amen.

Prayer to the Holy Spirit
O Holy Spirit, beloved of my soul, I adore you. Enlighten me, guide me, strengthen me, console me. Tell me what I should do . . . give me your orders. I promise to submit myself to all that you desire of me and to accept all you permit to happen to me. Let me only know your will. Amen.

Prayer to Your Guardian Angel
Angel of God, my guardian dear, to whom God's love commits me here, ever this day be at my side, to light and guard, to rule and guide. Amen.

Direction of Intention
My God, I give you this day. I offer you, now, all of the good that I shall do and I promise to accept, for love of you, all of the difficulty that I shall meet. Help me to conduct myself during this day

in a manner pleasing to you. Amen.

St. Francis de Sales

Fragrance Prayer

Dear Jesus, help me to spread your fragrance everywhere I go. Flood my soul with your spirit and life. Penetrate and possess my whole being so utterly that all my life may be only a radiance of yours. Shine through me, and be so in me that every soul I come in contact with may feel your presence in my soul. Let them look up and see no longer me but only you, dear Jesus! Stay with me, and then I shall begin to shine as you shine; so to shine as to be a light to others. The light, O Lord, will be all from you; none of it will be mine. It will be you, shining on others through me. Let me thus praise you in the way you love best: by shining on those around me. Let me preach you without preaching, not by words but by my example, by the catching force, the sympathetic influence of what I do, the evident fullness of the love my heart bears to you. Amen.

John Henry Cardinal Newman

Daily Prayer to Our Blessed Mother

[This devotion is prayed daily to our Blessed Mother, asking protection from evil and especially as a protection from sins against the virtue of purity.]

Mary, loving daughter of God the Father, I give my soul to your care. Protect the life of God in my soul. Do not let me lose it by sin. Protect my mind and my will so that all my thoughts and desires will be pleasing to God.

Hail Mary, full of grace; the Lord is with thee. Blessed art thou among women, and blessed is the fruit of thy womb, Jesus. Holy Mary, Mother of God, pray for us sinners, now and at the hour of our death. Amen.

Mary, loving Mother of God the Son, I give my heart to your care. Let me love you with all my heart. Let me always try to love my neighbor. And help me avoid friends who might lead me away from Jesus and into a life of sin.

Hail Mary . . .

Mary, loving spouse of the Holy Spirit, I give my body to your care. Let me always remember that my body is a home for the Holy Spirit who dwells in me. Let me never sin against him by any impure actions, alone or with others, against the virtue of purity.

Hail Mary . . .

Prayer of Consecration to Mary

I; (Name), an unfaithful sinner, renew and ratify today through you my baptismal promises. I renounce forever Satan, his empty promises, and his evil designs, and I give myself completely to Jesus Christ, the incarnate Wisdom, to carry my cross after him for the rest of my life, and to be more faithful to him than I have been till now.

This day, with the whole court of heaven as witness, I choose you, Mary, as my Mother and Queen. I surrender and consecrate myself to you, body and soul, with all that I possess, both spiritual and material, even including the spiritual value of all my actions, past, present, and to come. I give you the full right to dispose of me and all that belongs to me, without any reservations, in whatever way you please, for the greater glory of God in time and throughout eternity. Amen.

St. Louis DeMontfort

Prayers to the holy Spirit

The Holy Spirit longs to find the gates of our heart so that he may enter in and dwell there and sanctify it; and he goes round about to all the gates to see where he may enter.

St. Ephraim the Syrian

For God did not call us to impurity but to holiness. Therefore, whoever disregards this, disregards not a human being, but God, who gives his Holy Spirit to you.

1 Thess. 4:7–8 (NAB)

Prayers

Prayer to the Holy Spirit

Breathe in me, O Holy Spirit, that my thoughts may all be holy. Act in me, O Holy Spirit, that my

work, too, may be holy. Draw my heart, O Holy
Spirit, that I love but what is holy. Strengthen me,
O Holy Spirit, to defend all that is holy. Guard
me, then, O Holy Spirit, that I always may be holy.
Amen.

St. Augustine of Hippo

Prayer for the Gifts of the Holy Spirit

Holy Spirit, divine Consoler, I adore you as my true
God, with God the Father and God the Son. I adore
you and unite myself to the adoration you receive
from the angels and saints. I give you my heart,
and I offer my ardent thanksgiving for all the grace
which you never cease to bestow on me. O Giver
of all supernatural gifts, who filled the soul of the
Blessed Virgin Mary, Mother of God, with such im-
mense favors, I beg you to visit me with your grace
and your love and to grant me the gift of holy *fear*
so that it may act on me as a check to prevent me
from falling back into my past sins, for which I beg
pardon. Grant me the gift of *piety* so that I may
serve you for the future with increased fervor, follow
with more promptness your holy inspirations, and
observe your divine precepts with greater fidelity.

Grant me the gift of **knowledge** so that I may know the things of God and, enlightened by your holy teaching, may walk, without deviation, in the path of eternal salvation. Grant me the gift of *fortitude* so that I may overcome courageously all the assaults of the devil and all the dangers of this world that threaten the salvation of my soul. Grant me the gift of *counsel* so that I may choose what is more conducive to my spiritual advancement and may discover the wiles and snares of the tempter. Grant me the gift of **understanding** so that I may apprehend the divine mysteries and by contemplation of heavenly things detach my thoughts and affections from the vain things of this miserable world. Grant me the gift of **wisdom** so that I may rightly direct all my actions, referring them to God as my last end so that, having loved him and served him in this life, I may have the happiness of possessing him eternally in the next. Amen.

St. Alphonsus de Liguori

Prayer to the Holy Spirit
Come, Holy Spirit, enlighten my understanding to know your commands; strengthen my heart against

the wiles of the enemy: inflame my will. . . . I have heard your voice, and I don't want to harden my heart by resisting, by saying, "Later . . . tomorrow." *Nunc Coepi!* Now! Lest there be no tomorrow for me! O Spirit of truth and wisdom, Spirit of understanding and counsel, Spirit of joy and peace! I want what you want, I want it because you want it, I want it as you want it, I want it when you want it. Amen.

St. Josemaria Escriva

Veni, Sancte Spiritus

Come, Holy Spirit, fill the hearts of your faithful and enkindle in them the fire of your love. Send forth your Spirit, and they shall be created, and you shall renew the face of the earth.

Let us pray: O God, who instructs the hearts the faithful, grant that by the same Spirit, we may become truly wise and ever rejoice in his consolations, through the same Christ our Lord. Amen.

Prayers to Mary

If ever you feel distressed during your day, call upon our Lady. Just say this simple prayer: Mary, Mother of Jesus, please be a mother to me now.

Bl. Teresa of Calcutta (Mother Teresa)

My desire is for the young people of the entire world to come closer to Mary. She is the bearer of an indelible youthfulness and beauty that never wanes. May young people have increasing confidence in her, and may they entrust the life just opening before them to her.

Pope John Paul II

Let us ask our Lady to give us her heart, so beautiful, so pure, so immaculate, so full of love and

humility, that we may be able to receive Jesus in
the bread of life, love him as she loved him, and
serve him in the distressing disguise of the poorest
of the poor.

Bl. Teresa of Calcutta (Mother Teresa)

The formation and the education of the great
saints who will come at the end of the world are
reserved to her. . . . When the Holy Spirit, her
spouse, finds Mary in a soul, he hastens there and
enters fully into it. He gives himself generously to
that soul according to the place it has given to his
spouse.

St. Louis de Montfort

All generations will call me blessed.

Luke 1:48

Prayers

Rosary
The rosary is an ancient prayer of the Church, recom-
mended by countless saints. Pope Adrian VI referred to
it as "the scourge of the devil."

The rosary is a powerful weapon. Use it with confidence and you'll be amazed at the results.

Say the holy rosary. Blessed be that monotony of Hail Marys that purifies the monotony of your sins. . . . If you say the holy rosary every day with a spirit of faith and love, our Lady will make sure she leads you very far along her Son's path.

St. Josemaria Escriva

When the Hail Mary is well said—that is, with attention, devotion, and humility—it is, according to the saints, the enemy of Satan, putting him to flight; it is the hammer that crushes him, a source of holiness for souls, a joy to the angels, and a sweet melody for the devout. It is the canticle of the New Testament, a delight for Mary, and glory for the most Blessed Trinity. The Hail Mary is dew falling from heaven to make the soul fruitful. It is a pure kiss of love we give to Mary. It is a crimson rose, a precious pearl that we offer to her. . . . But say the rosary too and, if time permits, all its fifteen decades, every day. Then when death draws near, you will bless the day and hour when you took to heart what I told you, for having sown

the blessings of Jesus and Mary, you will reap the
eternal blessings in heaven.

St. Louis de Montfort

Although the rosary is a simple prayer, many people
find it difficult to stay focused while praying it. Even
St. Therese said, "Try as I will, I cannot meditate
on the mysteries of the rosary. I just cannot fix my
mind on them." So, do not be discouraged or feel
alone if you struggle in prayer. In order to overcome
distractions, St. Josemaria offers a challenge:

> You always leave the rosary for later, and you
> end up not saying it at all because you are sleepy.
> If there is no other time, say it in the street
> without letting anybody notice it. It will, more-
> over, help you to have presence of God.

How to Pray the Rosary
To pray the rosary, begin with the sign of the cross:

> In the name of the Father, and of the Son, and
> of the Holy Spirit. Amen.

On the crucifix, pray the Apostles' Creed:

I believe in God, the Father Almighty, Creator of heaven and earth, and in Jesus Christ, his only Son, our Lord, who was conceived by the Holy Spirit, born of the Virgin Mary, suffered under Pontius Pilate, was crucified, died, and was buried. He descended into hell; on the third day he arose from the dead; he ascended into heaven and is seated at the right hand of the Father Almighty; thence he shall come to judge the living and the dead. I believe in the Holy Spirit, the Holy Catholic Church, the communion of saints, the forgiveness of sins, the resurrection of the body, and life everlasting. Amen.

On the first bead, pray an Our Father (for the intentions of the pope):

Our Father, who art in heaven, hallowed be thy name. Thy kingdom come; thy will be done on earth as it is in heaven. Give us this day our daily bread and forgive us our trespasses, as we forgive those who trespass against us. And lead

us not into temptation but deliver us from evil.
Amen.

On the next three beads, pray a Hail Mary on each
(for faith, hope, and charity).

Then, pray the Glory Be:

Glory be to the Father and to the Son and to the
Holy Spirit, as it was in the beginning, is now,
and ever shall be, world without end. Amen.

For the rest of the rosary, you will pray an Our Father on the large beads, followed by ten Hail Marys,
a Glory Be, and the Fatima Prayer. Depending on
which day of the week it is, you can meditate on a
different mystery in the life of Christ (see below).

At the end of the rosary, pray the Hail, Holy
Queen:

Hail, holy queen, Mother of mercy! Our life,
our sweetness, and our hope! To thee do we cry,
poor banished children of Eve; to thee do we
send up our sighs, mourning, and weeping in
this valley of tears. Turn, then, most gracious

Advocate, thine eyes of mercy toward us; and after this our exile show unto us the blessed fruit of thy womb, Jesus. O clement, O loving, O sweet Virgin Mary.

Pray for us, O holy Mother of God.

That we may be made worthy of the promises of Christ.

Possible Additions

It is common to include the Fatima prayer after each Glory Be:

O my Jesus, forgive us our sins; save of us from the fires of hell; lead all souls to heaven, especially those who are in most need of thy mercy.

It is also common to conclude the rosary with the Prayer to St. Michael:

St. Michael the Archangel, defend us in battle. Be our protection against the wickedness and snares of the devil. May God rebuke him, we humbly pray, and do thou, O prince of the heavenly host, by the power of God, cast into hell Satan and all the evil spirits who prowl about the world seeking the ruin of souls. Amen.

The Joyful Mysteries

(Monday and Saturday)

The Annunciation: The angel Gabriel invites Mary to be the mother of Jesus.

The Visitation: Mary visits Elizabeth, who is pregnant with St. John the Baptist.

The Birth of Christ: Mary gives birth to Jesus in Bethlehem.

The Presentation: Mary and Joseph present Jesus in the temple.

The Finding in the Temple: Mary and Joseph find the child Jesus questioning the teachers in the temple.

The Luminous Mysteries

(Thursday)

The Baptism in the Jordan: St. John the Baptist baptizes Jesus.

The Wedding Feast at Cana: Jesus performs his first public miracle.

The Proclamation of the Kingdom: Jesus announces the gospel through his public ministry.

The Transfiguration: Jesus appears with Moses and Elijah in glory.

The Last Supper: Jesus celebrates the first Mass.

The Sorrowful Mysteries
(Tuesday and Friday)
The Agony in the Garden: Jesus fears his death but accepts the Father's will.

The Scourging: Jesus is beaten and scourged at the pillar.

The Crowning with Thorns: Jesus is mocked and given a crown of thorns.

The Carrying of the Cross: Jesus carries his cross to Calvary.

The Crucifixion: Jesus suffers and dies for our sins.

The Glorious Mysteries
(Wednesday and Sunday)
The Resurrection: Jesus rises from the dead.

The Ascension: Jesus ascends into heaven in the presence of his apostles.

The Descent of the Holy Spirit: The Holy Spirit descends upon Mary and the apostles.

The Assumption: Mary is taken bodily into heaven at the end of her earthly life.

The Coronation: Mary is crowned Queen of heaven and earth.

Memorare

Remember, O most gracious Virgin Mary, that never was it known that anyone who fled to thy protection, implored thy help, or sought thy intercession was left unaided. Inspired by this confidence, I fly unto thee, O Virgin of virgins my Mother; to thee do I come, before thee I stand, sinful and sorrowful. O Mother of the Word Incarnate, despise not my petitions but in thy mercy hear and answer me. Amen.

Angelus

(Traditionally, the Angelus is said at 6:00 A.M., noon, and 6:00 P.M.)

The Angel of the Lord declared unto Mary.

And she conceived of the Holy Spirit.

Hail Mary . . .

Behold the handmaid of the Lord.

Be it done unto me according to thy word.

Hail Mary . . .

And the Word was made flesh.

And dwelt among us.

Hail Mary . . .

Pray for us, O holy Mother of God, that we may be made worthy of the promises of Christ.

Let us pray: Pour forth, we beseech thee, O Lord, thy grace into our hearts; that we, to whom the incarnation of Christ, thy Son, was made known by the message of an angel, may by his passion and cross be brought to the glory of his Resurrection. Through the same Christ our Lord. Amen.

Seven Sorrows of Mary

(To honor the seven sorrows of Mary, St. Bridget encouraged the faithful to say seven Hail Marys while meditating on her sufferings.)

1. The prophecy of Simeon
2. The flight into Egypt
3. The loss of the child Jesus in the temple
4. The meeting of Jesus and Mary on the way of the cross

5. The Crucifixion
6. The taking down of the body of Jesus from the cross
7. The burial of Jesus

Prayer Praising Mary, the Mother of Jesus

Hail, holy lady, most holy queen, Mary, Mother of God, ever virgin. You were chosen by the most high Father in heaven, consecrated by him, with his most holy beloved Son and the Holy Spirit, the Comforter. On you descended and still remains all the fullness of grace and every good. Hail, his palace. Hail, his tabernacle. Hail, his robe. Hail, his handmaid. Hail, his Mother. And hail, all holy virtues, who, by grace and inspiration of the Holy Spirit, are poured into the hearts of the faithful so that from their faithless state they may be made faithful servants of God through you. Amen.

St. Francis of Assisi

Prayer of Self-Commendation to Mary

O Holy Mary, my lady, into your blessed trust and safekeeping and into the depths of your mercy, I commend my soul and body this day, every day of my life, and at the hour of my death. To you I entrust all my hopes and consolations, all my trials and miseries, my life and the end of my life. By your most holy intercession and by your merits, may all my actions be directed and disposed according to your will and the will of your divine Son. Amen.

St. Aloysius Gonzaga

Prayer to Our Lady

Blessed is the man who loves thy name, O Mary. Yes, truly blessed is he who loves thy sweet name, O Mother of God! Thy name is so glorious and admirable that no one who remembers it has any fears at the hour of death. I ask thee, O Mary, for the glory of thy name, to come and meet my soul when it is departing from this world and to take it in thy arms. Amen.

St. Bonaventure

Prayer to Our Lady of the Miraculous Medal
Virgin Mother of God, Mary Immaculate, I unite myself to you under your title of Our Lady of the Miraculous Medal. May this medal be for me a sure sign of your motherly affection for me and a constant reminder of my filial duties toward you. While wearing it, may I be blessed by your loving protection and preserved in the grace of your Son. Most powerful Virgin, Mother of our Savior, keep me close to you every moment of my life, so that like you I may live and act according to the example of your Son. Amen.

Prayer to Our Lady of Guadalupe
Our Lady of Guadalupe, who blessed Mexico and all the Americas by your appearance to Juan Diego, intercede for the holy Church, protect the pope, and help everyone who invokes you in their necessities. O mystical rose, hear our prayers and our petitions, especially for the

particular one we are praying for at this moment [mention your request]. Since you are the ever Virgin Mary and Mother of the true God, obtain for us from your most holy Son the grace of keeping our faith, sweet hope in the midst of the bitterness of life, burning charity, and the precious gift of final perseverance. Amen.

Prayer to Our Lady of Lourdes

O Immaculate Virgin Mary, Mother of Mercy, you are the refuge of sinners, the health of the sick, and the comfort of the afflicted. You know my wants, my troubles, my sufferings. By your appearance at the grotto of Lourdes you made it a privileged sanctuary where your favors are given to people streaming to it from the whole world. Over the years countless sufferers have obtained the cure for their infirmities—whether of soul, mind, or body. Therefore I come to you with limitless confidence to implore your motherly intercession. Obtain, O loving Mother, the grant of my requests. Through gratitude for your favors, I will endeavor to imitate your virtues, that I may one day share in your glory. Amen.

Prayer to Our Lady of Fatima

Most holy Virgin, who hast deigned to come to
Fatima to reveal the treasures of graces hidden in
the recitation of the rosary, inspire our hearts with
a sincere love of this devotion, that meditating on
the mysteries of our redemption recalled therein,
we may obtain the conversion of sinners, the
conversion of Russia, and [mention your request],
which we ask of you in this novena, for the greater
glory of God, for your own honor, and for the
good of souls. Amen. Our Lady of the Rosary of
Fatima! Pray for us!

Totus Tuus Prayer

Immaculate Conception, Mary my Mother,

Live in me, Act in me,

Speak in me and through me,

Think your thoughts in my mind,

Love through my heart,

Give me your dispositions and feelings,

Teach, lead me and guide me to Jesus,

Correct, enlighten and expand my thoughts and
behavior,

Possess my soul,

Take over my entire personality and life, replace it with Yourself,

Incline me to constant adoration,

Pray in me and through me,

Let me live in you and keep me in this union always.

Pope John Paul II

Prayer of Consecration

Immaculata, Queen of heaven and earth, refuge of sinners and our most loving Mother, God has willed to entrust the entire order of mercy to you. I; (Name), a repentant sinner, cast myself at your feet humbly imploring you to take me with all that I am and have, wholly to yourself as your possession and property. Please make of me, of all my powers of soul and body, of my whole life, death and eternity, whatever most pleases you.

If it pleases you, use all that I am and have without reserve, wholly to accomplish what was said of you: "She will crush your head," and, "You alone have destroyed all heresies in the world." Let me be a fit instrument in your immaculate and merciful hands for introducing and increasing your glory to the maximum in all the many strayed and indifferent souls, and thus help extend as far as possible the blessed kingdom of the most Sacred Heart of Jesus. For wherever you enter you obtain the grace of conversion and growth in holiness, since it is through your hands that all graces come to us from the most Sacred Heart of Jesus.

Allow me to praise you, O sacred Virgin.

Give me strength against your enemies.

St. Maximilian Kolbe

Prayers to Saints

Follow the saints, because those who follow them will become saints.

Pope St. Clement I

Be imitators of me, as I am of Christ.

1 Cor. 11:1

Prayers

ST. JOSEPH

St. Joseph was the husband of Mary and the foster father of Jesus. He is the patron saint of fathers, families, and the universal Church.

Prayer to St. Joseph the Worker
Glorious St. Joseph, model of all who are devoted

to labor, obtain for me the grace to work in the spirit of penance in expiation of my many sins; to work conscientiously by placing love of duty above my inclinations; to gratefully and joyously deem it an honor to employ and to develop by labor the gifts I have received from God; to work methodically, peacefully, and in moderation and patience, without ever shrinking from it through weariness or difficulty to work; above all, with purity of intention and unselfishness, having unceasingly before my eyes death and the account I have to render of time lost, talents unused, good not done, and vain complacency in success, so baneful to the work of God. All for Jesus, all for Mary, all to imitate thee, O patriarch St. Joseph! This shall be my motto for life and eternity. Amen.

Pope St. Pius X

Prayer to St. Joseph
My beloved St. Joseph, adopt me as your child.

Take charge of my salvation. Watch over me night and day. Preserve me from occasions of sin. Obtain for me purity of body and soul and the spirit of true prayer. Win for me a spirit of sacrifice, humility and self-denial. Obtain for me a burning love for Jesus in the Blessed Sacrament and tender love for Mary, my Mother. St. Joseph, be with me in life, be with me in death, and obtain for me a favorable judgment from Jesus. Amen.

Prayer to St. Joseph
Guardian of virgins and fathers, holy Joseph, to whose faithful care Christ Jesus, innocence itself, and Mary, Virgin of virgins, were committed: I pray and beseech thee, by these dear pledges, Jesus and Mary, that free from all uncleanness, and with spotless mind, pure heart and chaste body, you make me ever more chastely familiar with Jesus and Mary all the days of life. Amen.

ST. MICHAEL THE ARCHANGEL
St. Michael cast Satan into hell and is the chief in the army of God's angels. He is the patron saint of soldiers and policemen.

Prayer to St. Michael the Archangel
St. Michael the Archangel, defend us in battle; be
our protection against the wickedness and snares
of the devil. May God rebuke him, we humbly
pray, and do thou, O prince of the heavenly host,
by the power of God cast into hell Satan and all
the evil spirits who prowl about the world seeking
the ruin of souls. Amen.

ST. THERESE
OF LISIEUX

*St. Therese was a Carmelite nun
who died at the age of twen-
ty-four. Known for her "little
way" of doing small things with
great love, she is the patroness of
foreign missions because she un-
derstood that "sufferings gladly borne for others convert
more people than sermons."*

**Prayer to St. Therese of Lisieux
(the Little Flower)**
Beloved Little Flower, your life reflected the image
of Christ through your joyful love for others even

amidst your physical suffering. Little Therese of the Child Jesus, please pick for me a rose from the heavenly gardens and send it to me as a message of love. O Little Flower of Jesus, ask God today to grant the favors I now place with confidence in your hands [mention specific requests].

St. Therese, help me to always believe, as you did, in God's great love for me, so that I might imitate your "little way" each day. Amen.

ST. MARIA GORETTI

St. Maria Goretti is the patron saint of the youth and of rape victims because she was martyred at the age of eleven while defending her purity.

Prayer to St. Maria Goretti

O St. Maria Goretti, who, strengthened by God's grace, did not hesitate even at the age of eleven to shed your blood and sacrifice life itself to defend your virginal purity, look graciously on the unhappy human race that has strayed far from the path of eternal salvation. Teach us all, and especially youth, with what courage and quickness we should flee for the love of Jesus anything that could offend him

or stain our souls with sin. Obtain for us from our
Lord victory in temptation, comfort in the sorrows
of life, and the grace that we earnestly beg of thee
[here insert intention], and may we one day enjoy
with thee the imperishable glory of heaven. Amen.

Our Father, Hail Mary, Glory Be to the Father . . .
St. Maria Goretti, pray for us!

ST. RAPHAEL THE ARCHANGEL

*St. Raphael the Archangel is the patron saint of chaste
courtship and of those seeking a spouse. We read about
him in the book of Tobit in the Old Testament.*

Prayer to St. Raphael the Archangel

Glorious archangel St. Raphael, great prince of the
heavenly court, you are illustrious for your gifts of
wisdom and grace. You are a guide of those who
journey by land or sea or air, consoler of the afflicted, and refuge of sinners. I beg you, assist me
in all my needs and in all the sufferings of this life
as once you helped the young Tobias on his travels.
Because you are the "medicine of God," I humbly
pray you to heal the many infirmities of my soul
and the ills that afflict my body. I especially ask of

you the favor [mention your petition] and the great grace of purity to prepare me to be the temple of the Holy Spirit. Amen.

Prayer to St. Raphael to Intercede for those Contemplating Suicide

Holy archangel Raphael, appointed by God to guide, protect, and heal, I entrust to you all people who at this moment are contemplating suicide. You guided young Tobias on his journey and protected him from the spirit of death, which sought to destroy his life. I ask you to protect all people from the road that leads to physical and spiritual death, especially those in most danger of despair and suicide. Just as you lead Tobias by the hand, lead them away from the sadness of addiction to peace and joy. O holy Raphael, whose name means, "God has healed," bring them the Lord's healing. Lord God, hear the prayer I make together with your faithful servant Raphael. Amen.

ST. JOSEPH OF CUPERTINO

St. Joseph of Cupertino is one of the patron saints of students, because although he had little education and

*poor reading and writing abilities, he had a great gift
of spiritual knowledge.*

Prayer for Students

O great St. Joseph of Cupertino who by your
prayers did obtain from God the grace to be asked
in your examinations the only questions you knew.
Grant me success in these examinations for which
I am now preparing. In return I promise to make
your name known and cause it to be invoked. O
great St. Joseph of Cupertino, grant my requests.
Amen.

ST. PEREGRINE

*As a youth, St. Peregrine stood in defiance of the Cath-
olic Church but converted upon meeting a saint. He
became a priest and later in his life was miraculously
cured of cancer. Therefore, he is the patron saint of
cancer patients.*

Prayer for Cancer Victims

O great St. Peregrine, you who have been called
"the Mighty" and "the Wonder-Worker" because
of the numerous miracles you have obtained from

God for those who have had recourse to you. For so many years you bore in your own flesh this cancerous disease that destroys the very fiber of our being and had recourse to the source of all grace when the power of man could do no more. You were favored with the vision of Jesus coming down from his cross to heal your affliction. Ask of God and our Lady the cure of these sick persons whom we entrust to you. Aided in this way by your powerful intercession, we shall sing to God, now and for all eternity, a song of gratitude for his great goodness and mercy. Amen.

ST. PHILOMENA

St. Philomena was a young virgin martyr from the early Church and the only saint who was ever canonized based only upon the power of her intercession from heaven. She is the patroness of youth and the innocent.

Prayer to St. Philomena

O great St. Philomena, glorious virgin and martyr, wonder-worker of our age, obtain for me purity of body and soul, purity of heart and desire, purity of thought and affection.

Through thy patience under multiplied sufferings, obtain for me a submissive acceptance of all the afflictions it may please God to send me and as thou didst miraculously escape unhurt from the waters of the Tiber, into which thou wert cast by order of thy persecutor, so may I pass through the waters of tribulation without detriment to my soul. In addition to these favors, obtain for me, O faithful spouse of Jesus, the particular intention I earnestly recommend to thee at this moment. O pure virgin and holy martyr, deign to cast a look of pity from heaven on thy devoted servant, comfort me in affliction, assist me in danger, and above all come to my aid in the hour of death. Watch over the interests of the Church of God and pray for its honor and well-being, the extension of the faith, the sovereign pontiff, the clergy, the perseverance of the just, the conversion of sinners, and the relief of the souls in purgatory, especially those dear to me. O great saint, whose triumph we celebrate on earth, intercede for me, that I may one day behold the crown of glory bestowed on thee in heaven, and eternally bless him who so liberally rewards for all eternity the sufferings endured for his love during this short life. Amen.

ST. FAUSTINA KOWALSKA

St. Maria Faustina Kowalska was a nun from Poland who had a deep interior life and love for Jesus. The Lord spoke to her, appeared to her, and inspired her to spread devotion to the mercy of God. It is through her that we have the Chaplet of Divine Mercy.

Prayer to St. Faustina Kowalska

Dear St. Maria Faustina Kowalska, I have come to know you as a friend. I ask you to plead to the Lord for me the prayer I ask of you. In times of doubt, dear friend, implore the Lord's mercy as you did so often here on earth, that I may remember who I am and to what his mercy has called me.

In times of fear, implore his mercy that I may ever remember to trust, and trust again, in joy and in the knowledge that God is preparing me for a beautiful mission.

Please pray, dear St. Maria Faustina Kowalska, that I may never forget that the abyss between my Lord and me has been bridged by his tender mercy. He will continue to be faithful and heal me of anything that stands in the way of his will.

My life is in his hands.

Thank you, dear friend. Pray with me the prayer our Lord taught you to spread throughout the world: Jesus, I trust in you! Remind all pilgrims of life that if our trust is great, there is no limit to Jesus' generosity. Amen.

ST. JOHN BOSCO

When St. John Bosco was young, he would observe tricks performed at a local circus and practice them on his own. As he perfected them, crowds would gather to see him and, while entertaining them, he would repeat to them the homily that he heard from Mass. He had a great love for the youth and devoted his life to them. He is a patron saint of students.

Prayer to St. John Bosco
St. John Bosco, you reached out to children whom no one cared for, despite ridicule and insults. Help us to care less about the laughter of the world and care more about the joy of the Lord. Amen.

ST. DOMINIC SAVIO

St. Dominic Savio was a pupil of St. John Bosco, and he died at the age of fifteen. He was known for his remarkable courage, innocence, and love for God. His motto was "Death, but not sin!" and his last words before dying were "What beautiful things I see!" St. Dominic is the patron of boys and juvenile delinquents.

Prayer to St. Dominic Savio
Dear St. Dominic, you spent your short life totally for love of Jesus and his Mother. Help youth

today to realize the importance of God in their lives. You became a saint through fervent participation in the sacraments. Enlighten parents and children to the importance of frequent confession and Holy Communion. At a young age you meditated on the sorrowful Passion of our Lord. Obtain for us the grace of a fervent desire to suffer for love of him.

We desperately need your intercession to protect today's children from the snares of the world. Watch over them and lead them on the narrow road to heaven. Ask God to give us the grace to sanctify our daily duties by performing them perfectly out of love for him. Remind us of the necessity of practicing virtue, especially in times of trial.

St. Dominic Savio, you who preserved your baptismal innocence of heart, pray for us.

ST. MAXIMILIAN KOLBE

St. Maximilian Kolbe was a Franciscan priest who was imprisoned by the Nazis in a concentration camp in Auschwitz, Poland. He gave his life as a sacrifice for a fellow prisoner and was known for his deep love of the Virgin Mary. Since he was martyred by means of lethal injection while saving a father, he is the patron saint of drug addicts and families.

Novena Prayer to St. Maximilian Kolbe

O Lord Jesus Christ, who said," greater love than this has no man, than that he lay down his life for his friends," through the intercession of St. Maximilian Kolbe, whose life illustrated such love, we beseech you to grant us our petitions [here mention your requests].

Through the Militia Immaculata movement, which Maximilian founded, he spread a fervent devotion to our Lady throughout the world. He gave up his life for a total stranger and loved his persecutors, giving us an example of unselfish love for all men—a love that was inspired by true devotion to Mary.

Grant, O Lord Jesus, that we, too, may give ourselves entirely without reserve to the love and service of our heavenly Queen in order to better

love and serve our fellow man in imitation of your
humble servant, St. Maximilian. Amen.

Three Hail Marys and a Glory Be.

ST. GEMMA
GALGANI

*St. Gemma died at the
age of twenty-five. In her
short life she was known
for her remarkable mod-
esty, holiness, and beauty.
She had an extraordinary
spiritual life, encounter-
ing her guardian angel often and bearing the stigmata
(the wounds of Christ). She is the patroness of those
who struggle with temptations.*

Prayer to St. Gemma Galgani

O St. Gemma, how compassionate your love for
those in distress, how great your zeal to help them.
Help me, also, in my present necessity and obtain
for me the favor I humbly implore if it be profitable for my soul. The numerous miracles and the
wonderful favors attributed to your intercession

instill in me the confidence that you can help me. Pray to Jesus, your Spouse, for me. Show him the stigmata that his love has given you. Remind him of the blood that flowed from these same wounds, the excruciating pain you have suffered, the tears you have shed for the salvation of souls. Place all this as your precious treasure in a chalice of love, and Jesus will hear you. Amen.

Our Father, Hail Mary, Glory Be.

POPE JOHN PAUL II

Pope John Paul II was born Karol Wojtyla. He was orphaned by the age of twenty-one after losing his mother and father as well as his brother. Instead of turning from God in his sufferings, he studied to become a priest and was called by God to become pope in 1978. His motto as pope was "Totus Tuus," meaning that he was "entirely yours" (Mary's).

Prayer for the Intercession of Pope John Paul II

O Blessed Trinity, we thank you for having graced the Church with Pope John Paul II and for allowing the tenderness of your fatherly care, the glory of the cross of Christ, and the splendor of the Holy Spirit to shine through him. Trusting fully in your infinite mercy and in the maternal intercession of Mary, he has given us a living image of Jesus the Good Shepherd and has shown us that holiness is the necessary measure of ordinary Christian life—the way of achieving eternal communion with you. Grant us, by his intercession and according to your will, the graces we implore hoping that he will soon be numbered officially among your saints. Amen.

Prayers for Confession

In failing to confess, Lord, I would only hide you from myself, not myself from you.

St. Augustine of Hippo

To the penitent he provides a way back, he encourages those who are losing hope! Return to the Lord and give up sin, pray to him and make your offenses few. Turn again to the Most High and away from sin.

Sir. 17:19–21 (NAB)

When You Come to Confession
Before we sin, the devil tells us that God is lenient and merciful toward our weakness. But after we sin, he tries to drive us into despair by convincing us that God would never love us again. In reality, we

should contemplate God as a judge before we sin and as a loving Father if we sin. This is a simple principle, but the devil deceives millions by reversing it. If we're tempted to despair after sinning, remember the words of St. John Vianney: "Our sins are nothing but a grain of sand alongside the great mountain of the mercy of God."

Do not avoid confession if you keep committing the same sins. Rather, follow the advice of St. Francis de Sales, who said, "Have patience with all the world, but first of all with yourself." Also, do not avoid confession because you fear that your sins are too bad to confess. The Bible tells us, "His mercies never come to an end; they are new every morning" (Lam. 3:22–23).

St. Maria Faustina Kowalska recommended three things to the person preparing for confession:

1. Sincerity and openness: "An insincere, secretive soul risks great dangers in the spiritual life, and even the Lord Jesus himself does not give himself to such a soul on a higher level."
2. Humility: "A soul does not benefit from the sacrament of confession if it is not humble.

Pride keeps it in darkness. The soul neither knows how, nor is it willing, to probe with precision the depths of its own misery. It puts on a mask and avoids everything that might bring it recovery."

3. Obedience: "A disobedient soul will win no victory, even if the Lord Jesus himself, in person, were to hear its confession."

By giving us the sacrament of reconciliation, God does not want to cause you embarrassment or humiliation. He wishes to comfort us. But we must allow him. When writing to the youth of the world, Pope John Paul II reminds us that "in order to see Jesus, we first need to let him look at us!"

Examination of Conscience

According to St. Ignatius Loyola, "There are five points in this method of making the general examination of conscience:

1. Give thanks to God for favors received.
2. Ask for grace to know your sins and to rid yourself of them.

3. Demand an account of your soul from the time of rising to the present examination. Go over one hour after another, one period after another. The thoughts should be examined first, then the words, and finally the deeds.
4. Ask pardon of God our Lord for your faults.
5. Resolve to amend with the grace.

Close with an *Our Father.*

Using the Ten Commandments to Prepare for Confession

I am the Lord your God; you shall have no strange gods before me.

Is God the center of your life, or do you let things such as money, work, your image, popularity, a relationship, pleasure, or superstition replace God as your chief concern?

Have you used magic, horoscopes, or psychics?

Are you indifferent or ungrateful toward God? If you have difficulties with the faith, do you make an effort to find answers?

You shall not take the name of the Lord your God in vain.

Have you used God's name to curse other people?

Have you been careless with his name, using it as a joke?

Have you used his name as an exclamation when you're angry or surprised?

Have you used obscene language?

Remember to keep holy the Lord's Day.

Do you honor God, especially on Sunday and holy days of obligation?

Have you deliberately, without just cause, missed Mass on these days, arrived late, or left Mass early?

Have you shown reverence at the mass by modest dress and behavior?

At Mass, do you pay attention to Christ and his sacrifice for you, or does your mind wander?

Have you received Communion while in a state of mortal sin?

Do you make Sunday a day of rest and avoid unnecessary work?

Honor your father and your mother.
Have you been disobedient, dishonest, or disrespectful to your parents?

Do you cause them unnecessary worry?

Do you treat your siblings with respect and love?

Do you show respect and obedience to those who have authority over you?

You shall not kill.
Do you respect human life from conception to natural death?

Have you ever been responsible or partly responsible for the death of another (including abortion)?

Have you been drunk?

Have you taken any illegal drugs?

Have you ever endangered your life or the lives of others by driving recklessly or driving under the influence of alcohol or drugs?

Have you hurt others through insults or gossip?

Could you repeat in front of Jesus the things you have said about others?

Have you hurt your own body?

You shall not commit adultery.

Have you misused your sexuality, through masturbation, pornography, pre-marital sex, prostitution, rape, homosexual acts, contraception, or any form of sexual intimacy that belongs only in marriage?

Have you looked at others with lust, or indulged in impure thoughts?

Do you watch television shows, listen to music, read magazines, or play games that are not pure?

You shall not steal.

Have you stolen from others?

Have you deliberately damaged the property of another?

Have you cheated anyone from having what was due to him?

Do you always respect public property?

Are you lazy or wasteful of your time? Do you work diligently, or do you spend your employer's time doing personal things?

Do you neglect the poor?

You shall not bear false witness against your neighbor.

Have you lied?

Have you damaged the reputation of another by unkind words, gossip, or negative humor?

Have you betrayed another by revealing secrets that were entrusted to you?

Have you cheated on exams? Do you act hypo-critically?

Do you brag?

You shall not covet your neighbor's wife.
Do you harbor thoughts of sexual desire for some-one's else's spouse, or for anyone who is not your husband or wife?

Do you put yourself in occasions of sexual temptation?

Do you expose others to sexual temptations through immodest dress, impure speech, or crude behavior?

You shall not covet your neighbor's goods.
Instead of delighting in God's generosity to you, are you jealous of the talents and possessions oth-ers have?

Do you wish the misfortune of others so that you will profit?

Are you selfish, envious, materialistic, or self-centered, failing to have concern for others?

Using the Beatitudes to Prepare for Confession (Matt. 5:3–12)

While the Ten Commandments mostly tell us what to avoid, the Beatitudes tell us what to become. By examining our Lord's Sermon on the Mount, you can take a deeper look at the state of your soul before confession.

Blessed are the poor in spirit, for theirs is the kingdom of heaven.
Do you trust God with all of your heart, preferring him to everything?

Do you abandon yourself to God's Providence, giving him your anxieties in exchange for his joy?

Blessed are those who mourn, for they shall be comforted.
Do you have real sorrow in your heart for your sins?

If you do not, do you at least pray for that?

Do you wallow in your own problems or seek

out and comfort those who are lonely, rejected, or suffering?

Blessed are the meek, for they shall inherit the earth.
Are you haughty and proud or humble like Christ?

If you are gifted in academics, sports, music, or some other talent, do you give God the glory?

Do you serve others?

Do you follow God in order to please him with a sincere heart, or are you self-seeking?

Do you look down upon certain people, or do you treat others with respect, attention, and love?

Blessed are those who hunger and thirst for righteousness, for they shall be satisfied.
Do you long for God's will to be done, or do you pursue your own interests apart from him?

Are you lukewarm in my faith, being satisfied with mediocrity?

Blessed are the merciful, for they shall obtain mercy.
Are you mindful of how much God has forgiven you, or are you quick to condemn and slow to forgive others the harm that they have caused you?

Are you resentful?

Are you sympathetic to the needs of others?

Do you pray and work for the salvation of souls?

Blessed are the pure in heart, for they shall see God.
Have you not only rejected thoughts of lust but prayed to have a pure heart and live a life of purity?

Have you glorified God with your body? Do you act like your body is a temple of the Holy Spirit?

Blessed are the peacemakers, for they shall be called sons of God.
Do you not only avoid causing harm but strive to bring peace and reconciliation into the lives of others?

Blessed are those who are persecuted for righteousness' sake, for theirs is the kingdom of heaven.
Do you have the courage to do the will of God?

If mocked for living according to God's laws, do you give in?

Blessed are you when men revile you and persecute you and utter all kinds of evil against you falsely on my account. Rejoice and be glad, for your reward is great in heaven, for so men persecuted the prophets who were before you. Do you spread the faith and refuse to compromise it?

Do you not only refuse to use the Lord's name in vain but seek to correct those who do?

Have you been ashamed of Jesus, or do you challenge your friends who are falling into sin?

How to Go to Confession

While some churches have confession available every day, most have the sacrament available on Saturdays or by appointment.

When you arrive, take some time to examine your conscience. Ask the Holy Spirit to help you to remember where you've fallen away from God. Using the methods above will help you to do this. You could also say a prayer for the priest before entering the confessional.

When you enter, the priest may begin by greeting you or reading Scripture. You may respond by saying: "Bless me, Father, for I have sinned. It has been [the number of days, weeks, months, or years] since my last confession." You may also use your own words if you like, but you should give the priest an idea of how long it has been since your last confession.

After stating your sins (including how often they occurred), it is good to add: "I am sorry for these sins and all the sins of my life." The priest will give you a penance—usually a prayer to say, a Scripture passage to read, or a charitable act to perform. He will then invite you to say an act of contrition. You may offer the following one or use your own words to express sorrow for your sins:

O my God, I am heartily sorry for having offended you, and I detest all my sins because of your just punishments. But I am sorry most of all because they offend you who are all good and worthy of all my love. I firmly resolve, with the help of your grace, to sin no more and to avoid the near occasions of sin. Amen.

You also might use a simple act of contrition such as "God, be merciful to me, a sinner" (see Luke 18:9–14).

After the priest sees that you are genuinely repentant, he will give you absolution, saying:

> God, the Father of mercies, through the death and resurrection of his Son has reconciled the world to himself and sent the Holy Spirit among us for the forgiveness of sins; through the ministry of the Church may God give you pardon and peace, and I absolve you from your sins in the name of the Father and of the Son and of the Holy Spirit.

Finally, the priest may say: "Go in peace." And you say: "Thanks be to God." Or he may say: "Give thanks to the Lord, for he is good." And you say: "His mercy endures forever."

Although these steps using the Ten Commandments and the Beatitudes may seem a bit intimidating, don't be worried about following a perfect formula. What God looks at is the sincerity of your heart.

Prayer for Your Priest before Confession
Heavenly Father, bless your priest who will hear my

confession. Fill him with your love and wisdom, that he may guide me closer to you.

Jesus Christ, the High Priest, bless your priest so that he may image your presence to all who come to him.

Holy Spirit, come into the heart of your priest and, for the sake of the Church, fill him with your many gifts.

Blessed Mother Mary, wrap your mantle around your priest and always keep him close to the heart of your Son, Jesus.

All the holy angels and saints, pray for us during this sacrament and always. Amen.

Prayer of Repentance

O my crucified God, behold me at your feet; do not cast me out now that I appear before you as a sinner. I have offended you exceedingly in the past, my Jesus, but it shall be so no longer. Before you, O Lord, I place all my sins. I have now considered your own sufferings and see how great is the worth of that precious blood that flows from your veins. O my God, at this hour close your eyes to my want of merit, and since you have been pleased to die for my sins, grant me forgiveness for them all, that I may no longer feel the burden of my sins, for this burden, dear Jesus, oppresses me beyond measure.

Assist me, my Jesus, for I desire to become good whatsoever it may cost; take away, destroy, utterly root out all that you find in me contrary to your holy will. At the same time, I pray you, Lord Jesus, to enlighten me that I may be able to walk in your holy light. Amen.

St. Gemma Galgani

Prayers for Mass

When you approach the tabernacle remember that *he* has been waiting for you for twenty centuries.

St. Josemaria Escriva

The bread that I will give is my flesh for the life of the world. . . . Whoever eats my flesh and drinks my blood has eternal life, and I will raise him on the last day. For my flesh is true food, and my blood is true drink.

John 6:51, 54–55 (NAB)

Prayers

Prayer before Mass

Almighty and ever-living God, I approach the sacrament of your only-begotten Son our Lord Jesus Christ. I come sick to the doctor of life, unclean to the fountain of mercy, blind to the radiance of eternal light, and poor and needy to the Lord of heaven and earth. Lord, in your great generosity, heal my sickness, wash away my defilement, enlighten my blindness, enrich my poverty, and clothe my nakedness. May I receive the bread of angels, the King of kings and Lord of lords, with humble reverence, with the purity and faith, the repentance and love, and the determined purpose that will help to bring me to salvation. May I receive the sacrament of the Lord's body and blood, and its reality and power. Kind God, may I receive the body of your only begotten Son, our Lord Jesus Christ, born from the womb of the Virgin Mary, and so be received into his mystical body and numbered among his members. Loving Father, as on my earthly pilgrimage I now receive your beloved Son under the veil of a sacrament, may I one day see him face to face in glory, who lives and reigns with you for ever. Amen.

St. Thomas Aquinas

Prayer before Holy Communion

Lord Jesus Christ, I approach your banquet table in fear and trembling, for I am a sinner and dare not rely on my own worth but only on your goodness and mercy. I am defiled by many sins in body and soul and by my unguarded thoughts and words. Gracious God of majesty and awe, I seek your protection, I look for your healing. Poor troubled sinner that I am, I appeal to you, the fountain of all mercy. I cannot bear your judgment, but I trust in your salvation. Lord, I show my wounds to you and uncover my shame before you. I know my sins are many and great, and they fill me with fear, but I hope in your mercies, for they cannot be numbered. Lord Jesus Christ, eternal king, God and man, crucified for mankind, look upon me with mercy and hear my prayer, for I trust in you. Have mercy on me, full of sorrow and sin, for the depth of your compassion never ends.

Praise to you, saving sacrifice, offered on the wood of the cross for me and for all mankind. Praise to the noble and precious blood, flowing from the wounds of my crucified Lord Jesus Christ and washing away the sins of the whole world. Remember, Lord, your creature, whom you have redeemed with your blood. I repent of my sins, and I long to put right what I have done. Merciful Father, take away all my offenses and sins; purify me in body and soul, and make me worthy to taste the holy of holies. May your body and blood, which I intend to receive, although I am unworthy, be for me the remission of my sins, the washing away of my guilt, the end of my evil thoughts, and the rebirth of my better instincts. May it incite me to do the works pleasing to you and profitable to my health in body and soul and be a firm defense against the wiles of my enemies.

St. Ambrose

Prayer before Receiving Communion

Lord, Jesus Christ my God, forgive the faults and sins that I, your unworthy servant, have committed from my youth to this day and hour, whether knowingly or in ignorance; whether by words, deeds, intentions or thoughts; and whether by habit or through any of my senses. By the prayers of your pure and Virgin Mother, make me worthy without condemnation to receive your precious, immortal, and life-giving mysteries for the forgiveness of sins and eternal life. May the Eucharist sanctify, enlighten, strengthen, and heal my soul and body and thus destroy my evil thoughts, intentions, and prejudices. For yours, Christ our God, is the kingdom, the power, the glory, the honor and worship with the Father and the Holy Spirit, now and forever and ever. Amen.

St. John Chrysostom

Offering before Holy Communion

Lord Jesus, I wish to receive you into my heart with all the ardor of love that the most fervent soul ever had for you. May I receive you with the purity, love, and joy of Mary. Amen.

Prayer after Holy Communion

Lord, Father all-powerful and ever-living God, I thank you, for even though I am a sinner, your unprofitable servant, not because of my worth but in the kindness of your mercy, you have fed me with the precious body and blood of your Son, our Lord Jesus Christ. I pray that this Communion may not bring me condemnation and punishment but forgiveness and salvation. May it be a helmet of faith and a shield of good will. May it purify me from evil ways and put an end to my evil passions. May it bring me charity and patience, humility and

obedience, and growth in the power to do good.
May it be my strong defense against all my enemies, visible and invisible, and the perfect calming
of all my evil impulses, bodily and spiritual. May
it unite me more closely to you, the one true God,
and lead me safely through death to everlasting
happiness with you. And I pray that you will lead
me, a sinner, to the banquet where you, with your
Son and Holy Spirit, are true and perfect light,
total fulfillment, everlasting joy, gladness without
end, and perfect happiness to your saints. Grant
this through Christ our Lord. Amen.

St. Thomas Aquinas

Prayer after
Holy Communion
Stay with me, Lord, for it
is necessary to have you
present so that I do not
forget you. You know how
easily I abandon you. Stay
with me, Lord, because I
am weak and I need your
strength, that I may not

fall so often. Stay with me, Lord, for you are my life, and without you, I am without fervor. Stay with me, Lord, for you are my light, and without you, I am in darkness. Stay with me, Lord, to show me your will. Stay with me, Lord, so that I hear your voice and follow you. Stay with me, Lord, for I desire to love you very much and always be in your company. Stay with me, Lord, if you wish me to be faithful to you. Stay with me, Lord, for as poor as my soul is, I wish it to be a place of consolation for you, a nest of Love. Stay with me, Jesus, for it is getting late, the day is coming to a close, and life passes. Death, judgment, eternity approaches.

It is necessary to renew my strength, so that I will not stop along the way, and for that, I need you. It is getting late and death approaches. I fear the darkness, the temptations, the dryness, the cross, the sorrows. O how I need you, my Jesus, in this night of exile! Stay with me tonight, Jesus, in life with all its dangers, I need you. Let me recognize you as your disciples did at the breaking of bread, so that the eucharistic Communion be the light that disperses the darkness, the force that sustains me, the unique joy of my heart. Stay with me, Lord, because at the hour of my death, I want to remain united to you, if not by Communion, at least by grace and love. Stay with me, Jesus. I do not ask for divine consolation, because I do not merit it, but the gift of your Presence, O yes, I ask this of you! Stay with me, Lord, for it is you alone I look for. Your Love, your Grace, your Will, your Heart, your Spirit, because I love you and ask no other reward but to love you more and more. With a firm love, I will love you with all my heart while on earth and continue to love you perfectly during all eternity. Amen.

St. Pio (Padre Pio)

Anima Christi

Soul of Christ, sanctify me.

Body of Christ, save me.

Blood of Christ, inebriate me.

Water from the side of Christ, wash me.

Passion of Christ, strengthen me.

O good Jesus, hear me.

Within thy wounds, hide me.

Separated from thee let me never be.

From the malignant enemy, defend me.
At the hour of death, call me
To come to thee, bid me,
That I may praise thee in the company
Of thy saints, for all eternity. Amen.

Prayers before the Blessed Sacrament

Jesus has made himself the bread of life to give us life. Night and day, he is there. If you really want to grow in love, come back to the Eucharist; come back to that adoration.

Bl. Teresa of Calcutta (Mother Teresa)

My TV is the tabernacle.

Bl. Teresa of Calcutta (Mother Teresa)

We must understand that in order "to do," we must first learn "to be," that is to say, in the sweet company of Jesus in adoration.

Pope John Paul II

This is my body.

Matt. 26:26

Prayers

Prayer before the Blessed Sacrament

My Lord Jesus Christ, who for the love that you bear to men, remain night and day in this sacrament full of compassion and of love, waiting, calling, and welcoming all who come to visit you. I believe that you are truly present in the sacrament of the altar. I adore you humbly, and I thank you for all the graces that you have bestowed upon me, in particular for having given me yourself in this sacrament, for having given me your most holy Mother Mary as my mediatrix, and for having called me to visit you in this church. I salute your most loving heart, and this for three purposes: first, in thanksgiving for this great gift; secondly, to make amends to you for all the outrages that you receive in this sacrament from all your enemies; thirdly, to adore you, by this visit, in all the places on earth in which you are present in this sacrament and in which you are least revered and most abandoned.

My Jesus I love you with my whole heart! I grieve

for having so often offended your infinite goodness. I promise, by your grace, never more to offend you and, as unworthy as I am, I consecrate myself to you completely, renouncing my entire will, my affections, my desires, and all that I possess. Do with me as you please and whatever you please with all that I have. All that I ask and desire of you is your holy love, final perseverance, and the perfect accomplishment of your will. I entrust to you the souls in purgatory, especially those who had the greatest devotion to you in the most Blessed Sacrament and to the most Blessed Virgin Mary. I also recommend to you all poor sinners. Finally, dear Savior, I unite all my affections with those of your most loving heart and I offer them, thus united, to your eternal Father, beseeching him in your name, because of your love, to accept them and to grant my petitions. Amen.

St. Alphonsus de Liguori

Hymn to the Blessed Sacrament
O sacrament most holy, O sacrament divine, all praise and all thanksgiving be every moment thine!

Prayer before the Blessed Sacrament
We adore you, O Lord Jesus Christ, in this church
and all the churches of the world, and we bless you,
because, by your holy cross you have redeemed the
world.

Prayer to Jesus
Lord, take me from myself and give me to yourself.

St. Catherine of Siena

Prayer to the Blessed Sacrament
May the Heart of Jesus in the Most Blessed Sacrament be praised, adored and loved with grateful
affection at every moment in all the tabernacles of
the world unto the end of time!

Divine Praises
Blessed be God.
Blessed be his holy name.
Blessed be Jesus Christ, true God and true man.
Blessed be the name of Jesus.
Blessed be his most Sacred Heart.
Blessed be his Most Precious Blood.

Blessed be Jesus in the most Holy Sacrament of the Altar.
Blessed be the Holy Spirit, the Paraclete.
Blessed be the great Mother of God, Mary most holy.
Blessed be her holy and Immaculate Conception.
Blessed be her glorious Assumption.
Blessed be the name of Mary, Virgin and Mother.
Blessed be St. Joseph, her most chaste spouse.
Blessed be God in his angels and in his saints.

Golden Arrow

May the most holy, most sacred, most adorable, most mysterious, and unutterable name of God be always praised, blessed, loved, adored, and glorified in heaven, on earth, and under the earth by all the creatures of God and by the Sacred Heart of our Lord Jesus Christ in the most holy Sacrament of the Altar.

[In 1843, a Carmelite nun of Tours said that this prayer was revealed to her as a reparation against blasphemy.]

Act of Consecration to the Sacred Heart of Jesus

I give myself and consecrate to the Sacred Heart of our Lord Jesus Christ, my person and my life, my actions, pains, and sufferings, so that I may be unwilling to make use of any part of my being other than to honor, love, and glorify the Sacred Heart. This is my unchanging purpose, namely, to be all his and to do all things for the love of him, at the same time renouncing with all my heart whatever is displeasing to him. I therefore take you, O Sacred Heart, to be the only object of my love, the guardian of my life, my assurance of salvation, the remedy of my weakness and inconstancy, the atonement for all the faults of my life and my sure refuge at the hour of death. Be then, O heart of goodness, my justification before God the Father and turn away from me the strokes of his righteous anger. O heart of love, I put all my confidence in you, for I fear everything from my own wickedness and frailty, but I hope for all things from your goodness and bounty. Remove from me all that can displease you or resist your holy will; let your pure love imprint your image so deeply upon my heart that I shall never be able to forget you or to be separated from you. May I obtain from all your loving kindness the grace of having my name written in your heart, for in you I desire to place all my happiness and glory, living and dying in bondage to you. Amen.

St. Margaret Mary Alacoque

Novena to the Sacred Heart

[This novena was prayed daily by Padre Pio for all of those who requested his prayers.]

O my Jesus, you have said: "Truly I say to you, ask and you will receive, seek and you will find, knock and it will be opened to you." Behold I knock, I seek and ask for the grace of [mention your request].

Our Father . . . Hail Mary . . . Glory Be to the Father . . . Sacred Heart of Jesus, I place all my trust in you.

O my Jesus, you have said: "Truly I say to you,

if you ask anything of the Father in my name, he will give it to you." Behold, in your name, I ask the Father for the grace of [mention your request].

Our Father . . . Hail Mary . . . Glory Be to the Father . . . Sacred Heart of Jesus, I place all my trust in you.

O my Jesus, you have said: "Truly I say to you, heaven and earth will pass away, but my words will not pass away." Encouraged by your infallible words I now ask for the grace of [mention your request].

Our Father . . . Hail Mary . . . Glory Be to the Father . . . Sacred Heart of Jesus, I place all my trust in you.

O Sacred Heart of Jesus, for whom it is impossible not to have compassion on the afflicted, have pity on us miserable sinners and grant us the grace that we ask of you, through the sorrowful and Immaculate Heart of Mary, your tender Mother and ours.

Say the Hail, Holy Queen and add: St. Joseph, foster father of Jesus, pray for us.

St. Margaret Mary Alacoque

Spiritual Communion

A spiritual communion is a prayer offered whenever you are unable to receive Communion or throughout the day whenever you desire the presence of God. St. John Vianney said, "A spiritual communion acts on the soul as blowing does on a cinder-covered fire that was about to go out. Whenever you feel your love of God growing cold, quickly make a spiritual communion."

Act of Spiritual Communion

O Jesus, I turn to the holy tabernacle where you live hidden in love for me. I love you, O my God. I cannot receive you in Holy Communion. Come nevertheless and visit me with your grace. Come spiritually into my heart. Purify it. Sanctify it. Render it like unto your own. Jesus, meek and humble of heart, make my heart like your heart.

Chaplet of Divine Mercy

Say unceasingly this chaplet that I have taught you. Anyone who says it will receive great mercy at the hour of death. Priests will recommend it to sinners as the last hope. Even the most hardened sinner, if he recites this chaplet even once, will receive grace from my infinite mercy. I want the whole world to know my infinite mercy. I want to give unimaginable graces to those who trust in my mercy . . . O, what great graces I will grant to souls who say this chaplet; the very depths of my tender mercy are stirred for the sake of those who say the chaplet. Write down these words, my daughter. Speak to the world about my mercy; let all mankind recognize my unfathomable mercy. It is a sign for the end times; after it will come the day of justice. While there is still time, let them have

recourse to the fount of my mercy; let them profit from the blood and water that gushed forth for them.

As often as you hear the clock strike the third hour, immerse yourself completely in my mercy, adoring and glorifying it; invoke its omnipotence for the whole world and particularly for poor sinners; for at that moment mercy was opened wide for every soul. In this hour you can obtain everything for yourself and for others for the asking; it was the hour of grace for the whole world.

The words St. Faustina Kowalska said
she received from our Lord

Let us then with confidence draw near to the throne of grace, that we may receive mercy and find grace to help in time of need.

Heb. 4:16

How to Pray the Chaplet of Divine Mercy

Using ordinary rosary beads, begin with the Our Father, the Hail Mary, and the Apostles' Creed.

On the large bead before each decade, pray:

Eternal Father, I offer you the body and blood, soul and divinity of your dearly beloved Son, our Lord Jesus Christ, in atonement for our sins and those of the whole world.

On the ten small beads of each decade, pray:

For the sake of his sorrowful Passion, have mercy on us and on the whole world.

After five decades, conclude with:

Holy God, Holy Mighty One, Holy Immortal One, have mercy on us and on the whole world. (Three times)

Jesus, I trust in you. (Three times)

Eternal God, in whom mercy is endless and the

treasury of compassion—inexhaustible, look kindly upon us and increase your mercy in us, that in difficult moments we might not despair nor become despondent, but with great confidence submit ourselves to your holy will, which is Love and Mercy itself. Amen.

Stations
of the Cross

We always find that those who walked closest to Christ, our Lord, were those who had to bear the greatest trials.

Bl. Teresa of Calcutta (Mother Teresa)

For I decided to know nothing among you except Jesus Christ and him crucified.

1 Cor. 2:2

How to Pray the Stations of the Cross
After meditating on each station, pray an Our Father, Hail Mary, and Glory Be. Then, "We adore thee O Christ, and we bless thee, for by thy holy cross thou hast redeemed the world."

First Station: Jesus is condemned to death

Second Station: Jesus is given his cross

Third Station: Jesus falls the first time

Fourth Station: Jesus meets his Mother

Fifth Station: Simon helps Jesus with the cross

Sixth Station: Jesus falls a second time

Seventh Station: Veronica wipes the face of Jesus

Eighth Station: Jesus meets the women of Jerusalem

Ninth Station: Jesus falls a third time

Tenth Station: Jesus is stripped of his garments

Eleventh Station: Jesus is nailed to the cross

Twelfth Station: Jesus dies on the cross

Thirteenth Station: Jesus is taken down from the cross

Fourteenth station: Jesus is buried in the tomb

Prayers for Specific Intentions

PRAYER FOR YOUR FAMILY

Where does love begin? In our homes. When does it begin? When we pray together. The family that prays together stays together.

Bl. Teresa of Calcutta (Mother Teresa)

Children, obey your parents in everything, for this pleases the Lord.

Col. 3:20

Prayer

Heavenly Father, you have given us a model of life in the Holy Family of Nazareth. Help us, O loving

Father, to make our family another Nazareth where love, peace and joy reign. May it be deeply contemplative, intensely eucharistic, and vibrant with joy. Help us to stay together in joy and sorrow through family prayer. Teach us to see Jesus in the members of our family, especially in their distressing disguise. May the eucharistic heart of Jesus make our hearts meek and humble like his and help us to carry out our family duties in a holy way. May we love one another as God loves each one of us more and more each day, and forgive each other's faults as you forgive our sins. Help us, O loving Father, to take whatever you give and to give whatever you take with a big smile. Immaculate Heart of Mary, cause of our joy, pray for us. St. Joseph, pray for us. Holy guardian angels, be always with us, guide and protect us. Amen.

Bl. Teresa of Calcutta (Mother Teresa)

PRAYER FOR YOUR PARENTS

Do not neglect your obligation to love your parents more each day, to mortify yourself for them, to pray for them, and to be grateful to them for all the good you owe them.

St. Josemaria Escriva

Whoever honors his father atones for sins, and whoever glorifies his mother is like one who lays up treasure. . . . With all your heart honor your father, and do not forget the birth pangs of your mother. Remember that through your parents you were born; and what can you give back to them that equals their gift to you?

Sir. 3:3–4; 7:27–28

Prayer

Lord and Savior, you have taught us to honor our fathers and mothers, and to show love and obedience toward them. From the depth of my heart I fervently pray to you, Jesus, my God: hear my prayer. Bless my parents who have raised me up with the help of your grace. Protect them from evil, harm and sickness. Grant them faith, health and joy. Bless all their works that they may give you honor and glory all the days of their lives. Amen.

PRAYERS FOR YOUR STUDIES

An hour of study, for the modern apostle, is an hour of prayer.

St. Josemaria Escriva

Prepare your words and you will be listened to;
draw upon your training, and then give your answer.

Sir. 33:4 (NAB)

Prayers

Prayer of a Student
Christ my Lord, the
Giver of light and wis-
dom, who opened the
eyes of the blind man
and transformed the
fishermen into wise
heralds and teachers of
the gospel through the
coming of the Holy Spirit, shine also in my mind
the light of the grace of the Holy Spirit. Grant me
discernment, understanding, and wisdom in learn-
ing. Enable me to complete my assignments and to
abound in every good work, for to you I give honor
and glory. Amen.

Prayer before Study
Creator of all things, true source of light and wisdom, lofty origin of all being, graciously let a ray

of your brilliance penetrate into the darkness of my understanding and take from me the double darkness in which I have been born, an obscurity of both sin and ignorance. Give me a sharp sense of understanding, a retentive memory, and the ability to grasp things correctly and fundamentally. Grant me the talent of being exact in my explanations and the ability to express myself with thoroughness and charm. Point out the beginning, direct the progress, and help in completion, through Christ our Lord. Amen.

St. Thomas Aquinas

Prayer to Our Lady of Studies

O Mary, Seat of Wisdom, so many persons of common intellect have made through your intercession admirable progress in their studies. I hereby choose you as guardian and patron of my studies. I humbly ask you to obtain for me the grace of the Holy Spirit, so that from now on I could understand more quickly, retain more readily, and express myself more fluently. May the example of my life serve to honor you and your Son, Jesus. Amen.

St. Thomas Aquinas

Prayer after Study

I thank you, Lord our God, that again on this occasion you have opened my eyes to the light of
your wisdom. You have gladdened my heart with
the knowledge of truth. I entreat you, Lord, help
me always to do your will. Bless my soul and body,
my words and deeds. Enable me to grow in grace,
virtue, and good habits, that your name may be
glorified, Father, Son and Holy Spirit, now and
forever. Amen.

PRAYER BEFORE
STUDYING THE BIBLE

Ignorance of Scripture is ignorance of Christ,
which no man can afford.

St. Jerome

How different the man who devotes himself to the
study of the law of the Most High! He explores the
wisdom of the men of old and occupies himself
with the prophecies; he treasures the discourses of
famous men and goes to the heart of involved say-
ings; he studies obscure parables and is busied with
the hidden meanings of the sages. . . . His care is

to seek the Lord, his Maker, to petition the Most High, to open his lips in prayer, to ask pardon of his sins. Then, if it pleases the Lord Almighty, he will be filled with the spirit of understanding; he will pour forth his words of wisdom and in prayer give thanks to the Lord, who will direct his knowledge and his counsel as he meditates upon his mysteries. He will show the wisdom of what he has learned and glory in the law of the Lord's covenant.

Sir. 39:1–3, 6–8 (NAB)

Prayer

Shine within my heart, loving Master, the pure light of your divine knowledge and open the eyes of my mind that I may understand your teachings. Instill in me also reverence for your blessed commandments, so that having conquered sinful desires I may pursue a spiritual way of life, thinking and doing all those things that are pleasing to you. For you, Christ my God, are my light, and to you I give glory together with your Father and your Holy Spirit, now and forever. Amen.

PRAYER OF SELF-OFFERING

Entrust yourselves entirely to God. He is a Father
and a most loving Father at that, who would rather
let heaven and earth collapse than abandon anyone
who trusted in him.

St. Paul of the Cross

I urge you therefore, brothers, by the mercies of
God, to offer your bodies as a living sacrifice, holy
and pleasing to God, your spiritual worship. Do
not conform yourself to this age but to be transformed by the renewal of your mind, that you may
discern what is the will of God, what is good and
pleasing and perfect.

Rom. 12:1–2 (NAB)

Prayer

I offer you, Lord, my thoughts: to be fixed on you;
my words: to have you for their theme; my actions:
to reflect my love for you; my sufferings: to be endured for your greater glory. I want to do what you
ask of me: in the way you ask, for as long as you
ask, because you ask it. I pray, Lord, that you enlighten my mind, inflame my will, purify my heart,

and sanctify my soul. Amen.

Pope Clement XI

PRAYER FOR FAITH

Humbly ask God to increase your faith. Then, with new lights, you'll see clearly the difference between the world's paths and your way as an apostle.

St. Josemaria Escriva

So shun youthful passions and aim at righteousness, faith, love, and peace, along with those who call upon the Lord from a pure heart.

2 Tim. 2:22

Prayer

O my God, Trinity whom I adore, help me to forget myself so entirely as to establish myself in you, unmovable and peaceful as if my soul were already in eternity. May nothing be able to trouble my peace or make me leave you, O my unchanging God, but may each minute bring me more deeply into your mystery! Grant my soul peace. Make it your heaven, your beloved dwelling and the place of your rest. May I never abandon you there, but may I be there, whole and entire, completely vigilant in my faith, entirely adoring, and wholly given over to your creative action.

Bl. Elizabeth of the Trinity

PRAYER FOR HOPE

Do not fear what may happen tomorrow. The same loving Father who cares for you today will care for you tomorrow and every day. Either he will shield you from suffering or he will give you unfailing strength to bear it. Be at peace, then, and put aside all anxious thoughts and imaginings.

St. Francis de Sales

Rejoice in your hope, be patient in tribulation, be constant in prayer.

Rom. 12:12

Prayer

O my God, I am so certain that you watch over those who hope in you, and that when we rely on you for everything we can lack for nothing, that I am determined to live in the future without worry, casting all my cares upon you. People may deprive me of my worldly goods and of my honor; illness can take away my strength and the means of serving you. I may even lose your grace through sin, but I shall never lose hope. I shall keep it until the last moment of my life, when the efforts of all the devils in hell to take it from me would be in vain. Others may hope for happiness from their riches or from their talents—they may rely on their purity of life, on the severity of their penances, on the alms they have given or the fervor of their prayers. As for me, O my God, in my very confidence lies all my hope.

St. Claude de la Colombiere

PRAYER FOR LOVE

[A young heart feels] a desire for greater generosity, more commitment, greater love. This desire for more is a characteristic of youth; a heart that is in love does not calculate, does not begrudge, it wants to give of itself without measure . . . There is no place for selfishness—and no place for fear! Do not be afraid, then, when love makes demands. Do not be afraid when love requires sacrifice . . . Real love is demanding. I would fail in my mission if I did not tell you so. Love demands a personal commitment to the will of God.

Pope John Paul II

Love is patient and kind; love is not jealous or boastful; it is not arrogant or rude. Love does not insist on its own way; it is not irritable or resentful; it does not rejoice at wrong, but rejoices in the right. Love bears all things, believes all things, hopes all things, endures all things. Love never ends.

1 Cor. 13:4–8

Prayer

I love you, O my God, and my only desire is to love you until the last breath of my life. I love you, O my infinitely lovable God, and I would rather die loving you than live without loving you. I love you, Lord, and the only grace I ask is to love you eternally. . . . My God, if my tongue cannot say in every moment that I love you, I want my heart to repeat it to you as often as I draw breath.

St. John Vianney

PRAYER FOR JOY

Act in such a way that all those who come in contact with you will go away joyful. . . . Go through life like a little child, always trusting, always full of simplicity and humility, content with everything, happy in every circumstance. There, where others fear, you will pass calmly along, thanks to this simplicity and humility.

St. Faustina Kowalska

If you keep my commandments, you will abide in my love, just as I have kept my Father's commandments and abide in his love. These things I have spoken to you, that my joy may be in you, and that your joy may be full.

John 15:10–11

Prayer

Lord Jesus, you have created for me a life full of triumph and tribulation. Help me to learn from each and every experience, for all things happen for a reason, and all things happen according to your almighty plan. In all humbleness, please bless me with a state of happiness; accepting with a smile all that you send into my life. For I know that my happiness pleases you, O Lord, and brings me closer to the joys of heaven. I ask this in the name of Jesus, whose love reigns forever. Amen.

PRAYER FOR GENEROSITY

I ask you one thing: Do not tire of giving, but do not give your leftovers. Give until it hurts, until you feel the pain.

Bl. Teresa of Calcutta (Mother Teresa)

God loves a cheerful giver.

2 Cor. 9:7

Prayer

Teach us to be generous, good Lord; teach us to serve you as you deserve, to give and not to count the cost, to fight and not to heed the wounds, to toil and not to seek for rest, to labor and not to ask for any reward save that of knowing we do your will.

St. Ignatius of Loyola

PRAYER OF ENTRUSTMENT

Every day we have to say yes. To be where he wants
you to be. Total surrender: If he puts you in the
street—if everything is taken from you and suddenly you find yourself in the street—to accept
to be put in the street at that moment. . . to accept whatever he gives and to give whatever he takes
with a big smile. This is the surrender to God: to
accept to be cut to pieces and yet every piece to
belong only to him. This is the surrender: to accept
the people that come, the work that you happen to
do. Today maybe you have a good meal and tomorrow maybe you have nothing. There's no water in
the pump? All right. To accept and to give whatever
he takes. He takes your good name, he takes your
health, yes. That's the surrender. And you are free
then.

Bl. Teresa of Calcutta (Mother Teresa)

Let those who suffer according to God's will do
right and entrust their souls to a faithful Creator.

1 Pet. 4:19

Prayer

Take, O Lord, and receive my entire liberty, my
memory, my understanding and my whole will. All
that I am and all that I possess you have given me:
I surrender it all to you to be disposed of according to your will. Give me only your love and your
grace; with these I will be rich enough and will
desire nothing more.

St. Ignatius of Loyola

PRAYER FOR PATIENCE

If I did not suffer simply from moment to moment, I would find it impossible to be patient; but
I look only at the present, forget the past, and am
careful never to anticipate the future. When we
surrender to discouragement or despair, it is usually because we are thinking too much of the past
or the future.

St. Therese of Lisieux

A patient man is better than a warrior, and he who
rules his temper, than he who takes a city.

Prov. 16:32 (NAB)

Prayer

Dear heavenly Father, praise be given to your holy name for your forbearance and mercy. You have dealt gently with your children in love. You have been patient with me in my humanness and stubbornness. Lord, through the work of your Spirit, prompt me to be more jubilant in hope, more patient in times of trouble, and more consistent in my prayer life. Teach me, Lord, to wait with faith and expectancy, and may my trials be seen as times for growth in grace. Through Christ our Lord, I pray. Amen.

PRAYER IN TIME OF SUFFERING

The everlasting God has in his wisdom foreseen from eternity the cross that he now presents to you as a gift from his inmost heart. This cross he now sends you he has considered with his all-knowing eyes, understood with his divine mind, tested with his wise justice, warmed with loving arms, and weighed with his own hands to see that it be not one inch too large and not one ounce too heavy for you. He has blessed it with his holy name, anointed it with his consolation, taken one last glance at you and your courage, and then sent it to you from heaven, a special greeting from God to you, an alms of the all-merciful love of God.

St. Francis de Sales

Cast all your anxieties on him, for he cares about you.

1 Pet. 5:7

Prayer

Jesus, do not leave me alone in suffering. You know, Lord, how weak I am. I am an abyss of wretchedness, I am nothingness itself; so what will be so strange if you leave me alone and I fall? I am an infant, Lord, so I cannot get along by myself. However, beyond all abandonment I trust, and in spite of my own feeling I trust, and I am being completely transformed into trust—often in spite of what I feel. Do not lessen any of my sufferings, only give me strength to bear them. Do with me as you please, Lord; only give me the grace to be able to love you in every event and circumstance. Lord, do not lessen my cup of bitterness, but only give me strength that I may be able to drink it all. Amen.

St. Faustina Kowalska

PRAYER IN TIME
OF DISCOURAGEMENT

Hear, and let it penetrate into your heart, my dear little son: Let nothing discourage you, nothing depress you. Let nothing alter your heart or your countenance. Also do not fear any illness or vexation, anxiety or pain. Am I not here who am your mother? Are you not under my shadow and protection? Am I not your fountain of life? Are you not in the folds of my mantle, in the crossing of my arms? Is there anything else you need?

Our Lady of Guadalupe to St. Juan Diego

Trust in the Lord with all your heart, and do not rely on your own insight. In all your ways acknowledge him, and he will make straight your paths.

Prov. 3:5–6

Prayer

Behold me, my beloved Jesus, weighed down under the burden of my trials and sufferings. I cast myself at your feet that you may renew my strength and my courage while I rest here in your presence.

Permit me to lay down my cross in your sacred heart, for only your infinite goodness can sustain me, only your love can help me bear my cross, only your powerful hand can lighten its weight. O divine King, Jesus, whose heart is so compassionate to the afflicted, I wish to live in you, suffer and die in you. During my life, be to me my model and my support. At the hour of my death, be my hope and my refuge. Amen.

PRAYER FOR TRUST IN GOD

What God wants of you . . . is that you should live each day as it comes, like a bird in the trees, without worrying about tomorrow. Be at peace and trust in divine Providence and the Blessed Virgin, and do not seek anything else but to please God and love him. There is an unshakable truth, a divine and eternal axiom, as true as the existence of the one God (would to God I could engrave it on your mind and heart!): "Seek first the kingdom of God and his justice and all the rest will be added unto you." If you fulfill the first part of this declaration, God, who is infinitely faithful, will carry out the second; i.e., if you serve God and his holy Mother faithfully you will want for nothing in this world or the next.

St. Louis de Montfort

My son, when you come to serve the LORD, prepare yourself for trials. Be sincere of heart and steadfast, undisturbed in time of adversity. Cling to him, forsake him not; thus will your future be great. Accept whatever befalls you, in crushing misfortune be patient; For in fire gold is tested, and worthy men in the crucible of humiliation. Trust God and he will help you; make straight your ways and hope in him. You who fear the LORD, wait for his mercy, turn not away lest you fall. You who fear the LORD, trust him, and your reward will not be lost. You who fear the LORD, hope for good things, for lasting joy and mercy. Study the generations long past and understand; has anyone hoped in the LORD and been disappointed? Has anyone persevered in his fear and been forsaken? Has anyone called upon him and been rebuffed? . . . Let us fall into the hands of the LORD and not into the hands of men, for equal to his majesty is the mercy that he shows.

Sirach 2:1-10, 18 (NAB)

Prayer

Jesus, I trust in you!

Jesus, I trust in you!

Jesus, I trust in you!

St. Faustina Kowalska

Padre Pio received the stigmata while praying before this crucifix

PRAYER BEFORE A CRUCIFIX

Whatever human nature and reason may say, without the cross there will never be any real happiness nor any lasting good here below until judgment day. You are having to bear a large, weighty cross. But what a great happiness for you! Have confidence. For if God, who is all goodness, continues to make you suffer, he will not test you more than you can bear. The cross is a sure sign that he loves you. I can assure you of this, that the greatest proof that we are loved by

God is when we are despised by the world and burdened with crosses. . . . If Christians only knew the value of the cross, they would walk a hundred miles to obtain it, because enclosed in the beloved cross is true wisdom, and that is what I am looking for night and day more eagerly than ever. . . . After Jesus, our only love, I place my whole trust in the cross.

St. Louis de Montfort

I have been crucified with Christ; it is no longer I who live, but Christ who lives in me.

Gal. 2:20

Prayer

Look down upon me good and gentle Jesus, while before thy face I humbly kneel and with burning soul pray and beseech thee to fix deep in my heart lively sentiments of faith, hope, and charity, true contrition for my sins, and a firm purpose of amendment, while I contemplate with great love and tender pity thy five wounds, pondering over them within me and calling to mind the words that David thy prophet said of thee my Jesus, 'They have pierced my hands and my feet, they have numbered all my bones."

PRAYER FOR COURAGE

Let nothing trouble you. Let nothing frighten you. Everything passes. God never changes. Patience obtains all. Whoever has God wants for nothing. God alone is enough.

St. Teresa of Avila

The righteous are bold as a lion.

Prov. 28:1

Prayer

The Lord is my shepherd, I shall not want; he makes me lie down in green pastures. He leads me beside still waters; he restores my soul. He leads me in paths of righteousness for his name's sake. Even though I walk through the valley of the shadow of death, I fear no evil; for thou art with me; thy rod and thy staff, they comfort me. Thou preparest a table before me in the presence of my enemies; thou anointest my head with oil, my cup overflows. Surely goodness and mercy shall follow me all the days of my life; and I shall dwell in the house of the Lord for ever.

Ps. 23

PRAYERS FOR MINISTRY

So neither he who plants nor he who waters is anything, but only God who gives the growth.

St. Paul

But how are men to call upon him in whom they have not believed? And how are they to believe in him of whom they have never heard? And how are they to hear without a preacher? And how can men preach unless they are sent? As it is written, "How beautiful are the feet of those who preach good news!"

Rom. 10:14–15

Prayer Before Leaving for the Apostolate

Dear Lord, the Great Healer, I kneel before You, since every perfect gift must come from You. I pray, give skill to my hands, clear vision to my mind, kindness and meekness to my heart. Give me sin-

gleness of purpose, strength to lift up a part of
the burden of my suffering fellow men, and a true
realization of the privilege that is mine. Take from
my heart all the guile and worldliness that with the
simple faith of a child, I may rely on You. Amen.

Bl. Teresa of Calcutta (Mother Teresa)

Prayer After Ministry

Lord Jesus, thank you for sharing with me your
wonderful ministry of healing and deliverance.
Thank you for Your work that I have witnessed
and experienced today. I realize that the sickness
and evil I encounter is more than our humanity
can bear. So cleanse me of any sadness, negativity
or despair that I may have picked up.

If my ministry has tempted me to anger, impatience, pride, or lust, cleanse me of those temptations and replace them with love, joy, and peace.
If any evil spirits have attached themselves to me
or oppress me in any way, I command them to depart—now—and go straight to Jesus Christ, for
Him to deal with as He will.

Come Holy Spirit, renew me, fill me anew with

your power, your life and your joy. Strengthen me where I have felt weak and clothe me with your light. Fill me with life.

And Lord Jesus, please send your holy angels to minister to me and my family—and to guard us and protect us from all attacks, sickness, harm, and accidents. And guard me on my trip home. I praise you now and forever, Father, Son and Holy Spirit!

Francis MacNutt

PRAYER TO DEFEAT THE WORK OF SATAN

Many who may seem to us to be children of the devil will still become Christ's disciples.

St. Francis of Assisi

The God of peace will soon crush Satan under your feet.

Rom. 16:20

Prayer

O divine eternal Father, in union with your divine Son and the Holy Spirit, and through the immaculate heart of Mary, I beg you to destroy the power of your greatest enemy: the evil spirits. Cast them into the deepest recesses of hell and chain them there forever! Take possession of your kingdom, which you have created and is rightfully yours. Heavenly Father, give us the reign of the Sacred Heart of Jesus and the Immaculate Heart of Mary. I repeat this prayer out of pure love for you with every beat of my heart and with every breath I take. Amen.

PRAYER FOR DETACHMENT

How many things we own that we do not give away because we feel so attached to them. It is better to have less in order to give it all to Jesus.

Bl. Teresa of Calcutta (Mother Teresa)

He who does not take his cross and follow me is not worthy of me. He who finds his life will lose it, and he who loses his life for my sake will find it.

Matt. 10:38–39

Prayer

My Lord and my God, take from me everything that distances me from you. My Lord and my God, give me everything that brings me closer to you. My Lord and my God, detach me from myself to give my all to you. Amen.

St. Nicholas of Flüe

PRAYER FOR PEACE

The Christian has a deep, silent, hidden peace, which the world sees not, like some well in a retired and shady place.

John Henry Cardinal Newman

Have no anxiety at all, but in everything, by prayer and petition, make your requests known to God. Then the peace of God that surpasses all understanding will guard your hearts and minds in Christ Jesus.

Phil. 4:6–8 (NAB)

Prayer

Lord, make me an instrument of your peace. Where there is hatred, let me sow love; where there is injury, pardon; where there is doubt, faith; where there is despair, hope; where there is darkness, light; where there is sadness, joy. O divine Master, grant that I may not so much seek to be consoled as to console; to be understood as to understand; to be loved as to love. For it is in giving that we receive; it is in pardoning that we are pardoned; it is in dying that we are born again to eternal life.

St. Francis of Assisi

PRAYER FOR HUMILITY

Humility is to the various virtues what the chain is to a rosary. Take away the chain and the beads are scattered; remove humility, and all virtues vanish.

St. John Vianney

Do nothing from selfishness or conceit, but in humility count others better than yourselves. Let each of you look not only to his own interests, but also to the interests of others.

Phil. 2:3–4

Prayer

O Jesus! meek and humble of heart, hear me.
From the desire of being esteemed, *deliver me Jesus.*
From the desire of being loved,
From the desire of being extolled,
From the desire of being honored,

From the desire of being praised,
From the desire of being preferred,
From the desire of being consulted,
From the desire of being approved,
From the fear of being humiliated, *deliver me, Jesus.*
From the fear of being despised,
From the fear of suffering rebukes,
From the fear of being calumniated,
From the fear of being forgotten,
From the fear of being ridiculed,
From the fear of being wronged,
From the fear of being suspected,
That others may be loved more than I, *Jesus, grant
me the grace to desire it.*
That others may be esteemed more than I,
That in the opinion of the world, others may increase and I may decrease,
That others may be chosen and I set aside,
That others may be praised and I unnoticed,
That others may become holier than I, provided
that I may become as holy as I should.
O Jesus grant me:
knowledge and love of my nothingness,
the continuous memory of my sins,

the awareness of my selfishness,
the abhorrence of all vanity,
the pure intention of serving God,
perfect submission to the Will of the Father,
a true spirit of compunction,
blind obedience to my superiors,
holy hatred of all envy and jealousy,
promptness in forgiving offenses,
prudence in keeping silent about others' matters,
peace and charity towards everyone,
an ardent desire for contempt and humiliations,
the yearning to be treated like Thee,
and the grace of knowing how to accept it in a
holy way.

Holy Mary, Queen, Mother, and teacher of the
    humble, pray for me.

St. Joseph, protector and model of the humble,
    pray for me.

St. Michael, the Archangel, who was the first to
    bring down the arrogant, pray for me.

All Saints, sanctified by the spirit of Humility,
    pray for me.

Let us pray.

Lord Jesus Christ, though being God Thou didst

humble Thyself even unto death—and death on the cross—in order to be a constant example for us to confound our pride and self love. Grant us grace to imitate Thine example, so that by humbling ourselves as befits our wretchedness here on earth, we may be exalted and enjoy Thee in Heaven forever. Amen.

PRAYERS FOR PURITY

With all the strength of my soul I urge you young people to approach the Communion table as often  as you can. Feed on this bread of angels whence you will draw all the energy you need to fight inner battles. Because true happiness, dear friends, does not consist in the pleasures of the world or in earthly things, but in peace of conscience, which we have only if we are pure in heart and mind.

Bl. Pier Giorgio Frassati

Let no one despise your youth, but set the believers an example in speech and conduct, in love, in faith, in purity.

1 Tim. 4:12

Prayers

Prayer for Purity to the Sacred Heart
O Heart infinitely purer than the hearts of angels, the source of all purity, imprint on my heart a very special love of purity and a vivid horror of all that is contrary to it!

Prayer for Purity
Obtain for me a deep sense of modesty, which will be reflected in my external conduct. Protect my eyes, the windows of my soul, from anything that might dim the luster of a heart that must mirror only Christ-like purity. And when the "bread of angels" becomes my food in Holy Communion, seal my heart forever against the suggestions of sinful pleasures. May I be among the number of those of whom Jesus spoke, "Blessed are the pure in heart, for they shall see God." Amen.

PRAYER TO RESIST TEMPTATION

He did not say: You will not be troubled, you will not be tempted, you will not be distressed. But he said, "You will not be overcome."

St. Julian of Norwich

For this is the will of God, your sanctification: that you abstain from unchastity; that each one of you know how to take a wife for himself in holiness and honor, not in the passion of lust like heathen who do not know God.

1 Thess. 4:3–5

Prayer

Dearest Jesus! I know well that every perfect gift, and above all others that of chastity, depends upon the most powerful assistance of thy Providence and that without thee a creature can do nothing. Therefore, I pray thee to defend, with thy grace, chastity and purity in my soul as well as in my body. And if I have ever received through my senses any impression that could stain my chastity and purity, do thou, who art the supreme Lord of all my powers, take it from me, that I may with an immaculate

heart advance in thy love and service, offering myself chaste all the days of my life on the pure altar
of thy Divinity. Amen.

ACT OF CONSECRATION
TO MARY FOR PURITY

To be pure, to remain pure, can only come at a
price, the price of knowing God and loving him
enough to do his will. He will always give us the
strength we need to keep purity as something beautiful for him. Purity is the fruit of prayer.

Bl. Teresa of Calcutta (Mother Teresa)

Blessed are the pure in heart, for they shall see God.

Matt. 5:8

Prayer

O Immaculate Heart of Mary, Virgin most pure,
mindful of the terrible moral dangers threatening
on all sides and aware of my own human weakness,
I voluntarily place myself, body, and soul, this day
and always, under your loving maternal care and
protection. I consecrate to you my body with all its
members, asking you to help me never to use it as

an occasion of sin to others. Help me to remember that my body is "the temple of the Holy Spirit" and use it according to God's holy will for my own salvation and the salvation of others. I consecrate to you my soul, asking you to watch over it, and to bring it home safe to you and to Jesus in heaven for all eternity. O Mary, my Mother, all that I am, all that I have is yours. Keep me and guard me as your property and possession.

PRAYER TO REDEEM LOST TIME

It is Jesus that you seek when you dream of happiness; he is waiting for you when nothing else you find satisfies you; he is the beauty to which you are so attracted; it is he who provokes you with that thirst for fullness that will not let you settle for compromise; it is he who urges you to shed the masks of a false life; it is he who reads in your hearts your most genuine choices; the choices that others try to stifle. It is Jesus who stirs in you the desire to do something great with your lives, the will to follow an ideal, the refusal to allow yourselves to be ground down by mediocrity, the courage to commit yourselves humbly and patiently to improving yourselves and society, making the world more human and more fraternal.

Pope John Paul II

I will restore to you the years which the swarming locust has eaten.

Joel 2:25

Prayer

O my God! Source of all mercy! I acknowledge your sovereign power. While recalling the wasted years that are past, I believe that you, Lord, can in an instant turn this loss to gain. Miserable as I am, yet I firmly believe that you can do all things. Please restore to me the time lost, giving me your grace, both now and in the future, that I may appear before you in "wedding garments." Amen.

St. Teresa of Avila

PRAYER FOR HEALING

It is not in our power not to feel or to forget an offense; but the heart that offers itself to the Holy Spirit turns injury into compassion and purifies the memory in transforming the hurt into inter-cession.

Catechism of the Catholic Church 2843

The Lord is near to the brokenhearted, and saves the crushed in spirit.

Ps. 34:18

Prayer

Lord Jesus Christ, most holy Redeemer, you make all things new. Your word promises: Whoever is in Christ has become a new creation. The old has passed away; behold the new has come.

Renew us, and heal us with your love.

Make new my mind: Let me see life and death, time and eternity, this world and beyond, with the eyes of faith. Make new my will: Let me walk more loyally in the way of your commandments.

Renew us, and heal us with your love.

Make new my heart: Let me love you truly and love others for your sake. Make new, Lord Jesus, my whole life: Let there be no more sin, no more compromise, but only devotion to you.

Renew us, and heal us with your love.

I bring to you, dearest Lord, my life as it is—my hopes and dreams; my struggles and pains; my fears, anxieties, and addictions; my hurts; my talents; my achievements; my disappointments; and my sickness. I bring to you all whom I love. I entrust all to you and with confident faith. I take heart; for you make all things new.

Renew us, and heal us with your love. Amen.

PRAYER TO FORGIVE

All right: That person has behaved badly toward you. But haven't you behaved worse toward God?

St. Josemaria Escriva

Be merciful, even as your Father is merciful. Judge not, and you will not be judged; condemn not, and you will not be condemned; forgive and you will be forgiven; give, and it will be given to you; good measure, pressed down, shaken together, running over, will be put into your lap. For the measure you give will be the measure you get back.

Luke 6:36–38

Prayer

Lord, help us to forgive those who have hurt us. Help us to take the hurt and frustration and turn it into joy; because we know it is what you would have us to do. Help us to forgive so that you may forgive us. Heal the hurts and cleanse our minds. We thank you, Lord, that you can help us to forgive and close that chapter in our lives forever. In the name of Jesus. Amen.

PRAYER FOR A MERCIFUL HEART

Be always merciful as I am merciful. Love everyone out of love for me, even your greatest enemies, so that my mercy may be fully reflected in your heart.

Jesus to St. Faustina Kowalska

Blessed are the merciful, for they shall obtain mercy.

Matt. 5:7

Prayer

O Jesus, I understand that your mercy is beyond all imagining, and therefore I ask you to make my heart so big that there will be room in it for the needs of all the souls living on the face of the earth and the souls suffering in purgatory. Make my heart sensitive to all the sufferings of my neighbor, whether body or soul. O my Jesus, I know that you act toward us as we act toward our neighbor. Make my heart like unto your merciful heart; transform it into your own heart that I may sense the needs of other hearts, especially those who are sad or suffering. May the rays of mercy rest in my heart. Jesus, help me go through life doing good to everyone. Amen.

St. Faustina Kowalska

PRAYER FOR FORGIVENESS

The past must be abandoned to God's mercy, the present to our faithfulness, the future to divine Providence.

St. Francis de Sales

I will not remember your sins. . . . I have swept away your transgressions like a cloud, and your sins like mist; return to me, for I have redeemed you.

Is. 43:25; 44:22

Prayer

Have mercy on me, God, in your goodness; in your abundant compassion blot out my offense. Wash away all my guilt; from my sin cleanse me. For I know my offense; my sin is always before me. Against you alone have I sinned; I have done such evil in your sight that you are just in your sentence, blameless when you condemn. True, I was born guilty, a sinner, even as my mother conceived me. Still, you insist on sincerity of heart; in my inmost being teach me wisdom. Cleanse me with hyssop, that I may be pure; wash me, make me whiter than snow. Let me hear sounds of joy and gladness; let the bones you have crushed rejoice. Turn away your face from my sins; blot out all my guilt. A clean heart create for me, God; renew in me a steadfast spirit. Do not drive me from your presence, nor take from me your holy spirit. Restore my joy in your salvation; sustain in me a willing spirit. I will teach the wicked your ways, that sinners may return to you. Rescue me from death, God, my saving God, that my tongue may praise your healing power. Lord, open my lips; my mouth will proclaim your praise. For you do not desire sacrifice; a burnt offering you would not accept. My sacrifice, God, is a broken spirit; God, do not spurn a broken, humbled heart. Make Zion prosper in your good pleasure; rebuild the walls of Jerusalem. Then you will be pleased with proper sacrifice, burnt offerings and holocausts; then bullocks will be offered on your altar.

Psalm 51 (NAB)

PRAYERS OF ATONEMENT

It's a form of trade, you see. I ask God for souls and pay him by giving up everything else.

St. John Bosco

Whoever brings back a sinner from the error of his way will save his soul from death and will cover a multitude of sins.

Jas. 5:20

Prayers

Angels Prayer

Most Holy Trinity—Father, Son, and Holy Spirit—I adore thee profoundly. I offer thee the most precious body, blood, soul and divinity of

Jesus Christ, present in all the tabernacles of the world, in reparation for the outrages, sacrileges, and indifferences whereby he is offended. And through the infinite merits of his most Sacred Heart and the Immaculate Heart of Mary, I beg of thee the conversion of poor sinners.

Pardon Prayer

My God, I believe, I adore, I hope, and I love you. I beg pardon of you for those who do not believe, do not adore, do not hope, and do not love you.
[Taught to the three children by an angel in Fatima in 1916]

PRAYER TO KNOW GOD'S WILL

Prayer is not asking. Prayer is putting oneself in the hands of God, at his disposition, and listening to his voice in the depths of our hearts.

Bl. Teresa of Calcutta (Mother Teresa)

Behold, I am the handmaid of the Lord; let it be to me according to your word.

Luke 1:38

Prayer

Lord grant that I may always allow myself to be guided by you, always follow your plans, and perfectly accomplish your holy will. Grant that in all things, great and small, today and all the days of my life, I may do whatever you may require of me. Help me to respond to the slightest prompting of your grace so that I may be your trustworthy instrument. May your will be done in time and eternity, by me, in me, and through me. Amen.

St. Therese of Lisieux

PRAYER FOR DIRECTION

Confidently open your most intimate aspirations to the love of Christ who waits for you in the Eucharist. You will receive the answer to all your worries and you will see with joy that the consistency of your life, which he asks of you, is the door to fulfill the noblest dreams of your youth.

Pope John Paul II

For I know well the plans I have in mind for you, plans for your welfare, not for woe! Plans to give you a future full of hope. When you call me, when you go to pray to me, I will listen to you. When you look for me, you will find me. Yes, when you seek me with all your heart, you will find me with you, and I will change your lot.

Jer. 29:11–14 (NAB)

Prayer

I wait for you, O Lord; I lift up my soul to my God. In you I trust; do not let me be disgraced; do not let my enemies gloat over me. No one is disgraced who waits for you, but only those who lightly break faith. Make known to me your ways, Lord; teach me your paths. Guide me in your truth and teach me, for you are God and my savior. For you I wait all the long day, because of your goodness, Lord. Remember your compassion and love, O Lord; for they are ages old. Remember no more the sins of my youth, Remember me only in light of your love.

Ps. 25:1–7 (NAB)

PRAYER TO DISCERN ONE'S VOCATION

In the first place I say this: You must never think

that you are alone in deciding your future! And second: when deciding your future, you must not decide for yourself alone!

Pope John Paul II

At dawn let me hear of your kindness, for in you I trust. Show me the path I should walk, for to you I entrust my life. Rescue me, Lord, from my foes, for in you I hope. Teach me to do your will, for you are my God. . . . I am your servant.

Ps. 143:8–10, 12 (NAB)

Prayer

Almighty Father, you send the gift of your Holy Spirit for the building of your kingdom. With the help of this Spirit, give me the grace to listen to your call in my life. Give me strength and courage to do your will. Grant me wisdom and humility to choose your way even when I find it most difficult. Lord, bless all the faithful in your Church who are seeking holiness. But in a special way, watch over priests, brothers, and sisters. Help them to give themselves in joyful service that they may be signs of your presence among us. We beg you, Father, to fill our hearts with a burning desire to follow Jesus. May there be many, who offer their lives for the service of your Church, that all may come to know and love you. We ask this through Christ our Lord. Amen.

PRAYER FOR VOCATIONS

[Young people] know that their life has meaning to the extent that it becomes a free gift for others.

Pope John Paul II

The harvest is plentiful, but the laborers are few; pray therefore the Lord of the harvest to send out laborers into his harvest.

Matt. 9:37–38

Prayer

Jesus, High Priest and Redeemer forever, we beg you to call young men and women to your service as priests and religious. May they be inspired by the lives of dedicated priests, brothers, and sisters. Give to parents the grace of generosity and trust toward

you and their children so that their sons and daugh-
ters may be helped to choose their vocations in life
with wisdom and freedom. Lord, you told us that
the harvest indeed is great but the laborers are few.
Pray, therefore, the Lord of the harvests to send
laborers into his harvest. We pray particularly for
those called to serve as priests, brothers, and sisters;
those whom you have called, those you are calling
now, and those you will call in the future. May they
be open and responsive to the call of serving your
people. We ask this through Christ, our Lord. Amen.

PRAYERS FOR PRIESTS

Priesthood is the love of the heart of Jesus. When
you see a priest, think of our Lord Jesus Christ.

St. John Vianney

For though you have countless guides in Christ,
you do not have many fathers. For I became your
father in Christ Jesus through the gospel.

1 Cor. 4:15

Prayers

Prayer for Priests

Keep them, I pray thee, dearest Lord. Keep them, for they are thine. Thy priests whose lives burn out before thy consecrated shrine. Keep them, for they are in the world, though from the world apart. When earthly pleasures tempt, allure, shelter them in thy heart. Keep them, and comfort them in hours of loneliness and pain, when all their life of sacrifice for souls seems but in vain. Keep them, and remember, Lord, they have no one but thee, yet they have only human hearts, with human frailty. Keep them as spotless as the Host, which daily they caress; their every thought and word and deed, deign, dearest Lord, to bless.

Prayer for Priests

O Holy Father, may the torrents of love flowing from the sacred wounds of thy divine Son bring forth priests like unto the beloved disciple John who stood at the foot of the cross, priests who as a pledge of thine own most tender love will lovingly give thy divine Son to the souls of men.

May thy priests be faithful guardians of thy

Church, as John was of Mary, whom he received into his house. Taught by this loving Mother who suffered so much on Calvary, may they display a mother's care and thoughtfulness toward thy children. May they teach souls to enter into close union with thee through Mary who, as the gate of heaven, is specially the guardian of the treasures of thy divine heart.

Give us priests who are on fire and who are true children of Mary, priests who will give Jesus to souls with the same tenderness and care with which Mary carried the little Child of Bethlehem.

Mother of sorrows and of love, out of compassion for thy beloved Son, open in our hearts deep wells of love so that we may console him and give him a generation of priests formed in thy school and having all the tender thoughtfulness of thine own spotless love.

St. Therese of Lisieux

PRAYER FOR THE POPE

May the daily consideration of the heavy burden that weighs upon the pope and the bishops move you to venerate and love them with real affection and to help them with your prayers.

St. Josemaria Escriva

And I tell you, you are Peter, and on this rock I will build my church, and the powers of death shall not prevail against it.

Matt. 16:18

Prayer

May the Lord sustain and strengthen our Holy Father, give him happiness on earth, and not allow him to fall into the hands of his enemies. Lord, graciously hear his prayers, bless his endeavors, and fulfill his wishes, which have in view the honor and well-being of thy Church. Guide, enlighten, strengthen, and protect him so that he may worthily rule thy kingdom on earth at all times and attain to eternal life, together with the flock entrusted to him, thou who lives and reigns, world without end. Amen.

PRAYER TO END ABORTION

Any country that accepts abortion is not teaching the people to love but to use any violence to get what they want. That is why the greatest destroyer of love and peace is abortion.

Bl. Teresa of Calcutta (Mother Teresa)

If you remain indifferent in time of adversity, your strength will depart from you. Rescue those who are being dragged to death, and from those tottering to execution, withdraw not. If you say, "I know not this man!" does not he who tests hearts perceive it? He who guards your life knows it, and he will repay each one according to his deeds.

Prov. 24:10–12 (NAB)

Prayer

Heavenly Father, in your love for us, protect against the wickedness of the devil, those helpless little ones to whom you have given the gift of life. Touch with pity the hearts of those women pregnant in our world today who are not thinking of motherhood. Help them to see that the child they carry is made in your image—as well as theirs—made for eternal life. Dispel their fear and selfishness and give them true womanly hearts to love their babies and give them birth and all the needed care that a mother can give. We ask this through Jesus Christ, your Son, Our Lord, Who lives and reigns with you and the Holy Spirit, One God, forever and ever. Amen.

PRAYER FOR THE HOLY SOULS IN PURGATORY

The holy souls in purgatory. Out of charity, out of justice, and out of an excusable selfishness (they have such power with God!), remember them often in your sacrifices and in your prayers. Whenever you speak of them, may you be able to say, "My good friends, the souls in purgatory."

St. Josemaria Escriva

It was a holy and pious thought. Therefore he made atonement for the dead, that they might be delivered from their sin.

2 Macc. 12:45

Prayer

Eternal Father, I offer you the most precious blood of your divine Son, Jesus, in union with the Masses said today, for all the holy souls in purgatory, for sinners everywhere, for sinners in the universal Church, those in my own home and within my own family. Amen.

PRAYER FOR A
DEPARTED LOVED ONE

We have loved them during life; let us not abandon them until we have conducted them by our prayers into the house of the Lord.

St. Ambrose

The souls of the righteous are in the hand of God.

Wis. 3:1

Prayer

O gentlest heart of Jesus, ever present in the Blessed Sacrament, ever consumed with burning love for the poor souls, have mercy on the soul of thy departed servant. Be not severe in thy judgment but let some drops of thy precious blood fall upon the purifying flames, and do thou, O merciful Savior, send thy angels to conduct thy departed servant to a place of refreshment, light, and peace. Amen. May the souls of all the faithfully departed,

through the mercy of God, rest in peace. Amen.
Merciful Jesus, grant eternal rest.

Evening Prayers

When night comes, and you look back over the day and see how fragmentary everything has been, and how much you planned that has gone undone, and all the reasons you have to be embarrassed and ashamed: just take everything exactly as it is, put it in God's hands and leave it with him. Then you will be able to rest in him—really rest—and start the next day as a new life.

St. Teresa Benedicta of the Cross

At midnight I rise to praise thee.

Ps. 119:62

Prayers

Prayer for Daily Neglects
Eternal Father, I offer thee the Sacred Heart of

Jesus, with all its love, all its sufferings and all its merits.

First, to expiate all the sins I have committed this day and during all my life.

Glory be to the Father, and to the Son, and to the Holy Spirit, as it was in the beginning, is now, and ever shall be, world without end, Amen.

Second, to purify the good I have done poorly this day and during all my life.

Glory be to the Father . . .

Third, to supply for the good I ought to have done and that I have neglected this day and all my life.

Glory be to the Father . . .

Healing Prayer at Bedtime
Jesus, through the power of the Holy Spirit, go back into my memory as I sleep. Every hurt that has ever been done to me—heal that hurt. Every hurt that I have ever caused to another person—heal that hurt. All the relationships that have been damaged in my whole life that I'm not aware of—heal those relationships. But, Lord, if there is anything that I need to do—if I need to go to a person because he

is still suffering from my hand, bring to my awareness that person. I choose to forgive, and I ask to be forgiven. Remove whatever bitterness may be in my heart, Lord, and fill the empty spaces with your love. Thank you, Jesus. Amen.

Prayer at the End of the Day

Jesus Christ my God, I adore you and I thank you for all the graces you have given me this day. I offer you my sleep and all the moments of this night, and I implore you to keep me safe from sin. To this end I place myself in your sacred side and under the mantle of our Lady, my Mother. Let your holy angels surround me and keep me in peace, and let your blessing be upon me. Amen.

St. Alphonsus de Liguori

Prayer to Your Guardian Angel

Angel of God, my guardian dear, to whom God's love commits me here, ever this night be at my side, to light and guard, to rule and guide. Amen.

Evening Prayer to Our Lady

Mary, my dear Mother, I thank you for the special

protection you have provided for me throughout this day. Obtain for me the grace of being always faithful to my commitments. Let purity and sacrifice be my daily bread, humility and obedience my comfort, the tabernacle my relaxation, and you, dear Mother, the school where I learn to practice every virtue. I cannot praise Christ while I sleep, so offer him my heartbeats as fervent acts of love. Keep me free from any act or thought that could dishonor his regard for me, and give me your tender motherly blessing.

Prayer on Going to Bed

Visit this house, we beg you, Lord, and banish from it the deadly power of the evil one. May your holy angels dwell here to keep us in peace, and may your blessing be always upon us. We ask this through Christ our Lord. Amen.

Goodnight, Jesus

Goodnight, my Beloved; I rejoice at being one day closer to eternity. And if you let me wake up tomorrow, Jesus, I shall begin a new hymn to your praise.

St. Faustina Kowalska

Evening Examen

St. Ignatius Loyola recommended, "Before going to bed make a general examination of conscience, then . . . go to sleep with a good thought on your mind." How do we do this? Many people think of the examination of conscience as a way to merely focus on their sins. But when done properly, that is not the main focus. Fr. Michael Gaitley offers a helpful tool in his book *33 Days to Morning Glory*. In it, he recommends we use the acronym B.A.K.E.R. to remember the key points of this spiritual exercise.

First, because this is a time of prayer and not merely a mental exercise, place yourself in the presence of God and ask the help of the Holy Spirit. Then, begin.

B: Blessings. Call to mind the blessings that God has bestowed on you throughout the day, and praise and bless him for those gifts. These blessings may have come in the form of crosses as well as consolations. Thank God for both, and you will develop a spirit of gratitude. St. Ignatius taught that this is the most important of the five points.

Therefore, spend the most time on it.

A: Ask. Ask the Holy Spirit to help you recognize your sins.

K: Kill. It was our sins that crucified Jesus. Examine your day and look for places where you committed sins in your thoughts, words, or deeds, and where you sinned by the omission of good acts. Call to mind the times of desolation during the day. In moments of sorrow, did you turn from God toward false consolations? Did you forgive a person who harmed you? Did you accept the sufferings you experienced? Dwelling on such low points of the day might cause our spirits to feel heavy. This leads us to the next step.

E. Embrace. Allow God's love and mercy to embrace you. You may wish to call to mind the image of Divine Mercy, or the moment when John the Beloved apostle rested his head on Christ's heart. When you bring Jesus your brokenness, you give him the joy of being your savior. Take your time to dwell on this point without rushing to the next.

R. Resolution. Take what you have gained from this examination, and make resolutions focused on the next day. Consider the opportunities for virtue and vice that await you, and prepare your strategy to grow in grace.

Appendix
Recommended Reading

Many people find prayer difficult because their mind wanders, because they don't know what to focus on, or because they can't seem to hear God. One useful solution to all three of these difficulties is to use spiritual reading during your prayer time.

First and foremost, you should take time to read Sacred Scripture. Instead of starting on page one in Genesis and hoping to finish Revelation, begin with the four Gospels. A good second step would be to read any of the New Testament letters or Proverbs, Sirach, Wisdom, or Psalms from the Old Testament. Eventually, try to read all seventy-three books.

Outside of the Bible, we are blessed to have 2,000 years of saints to guide us. Their words are a treasure for anyone who desires to grow in the love of God. As St. Josemaria Escriva counseled, "Don't neglect your spiritual reading. Reading has made many saints."

Ten Great Books for Spritual Reading

Story of a Soul by St. Therese of Lisieux

Introduction to the Devout Life by St. Francis de Sales

True Devotion to Mary by St. Louis de Montfort

The Way, Furrow, and *The Forge* by St. Josemaria Escriva

Diary: Divine Mercy in My Soul by St. Maria Faustina Kowalska

The Spiritual Exercises by St. Ignatius Loyola

Interior Castle by St. Teresa of Avila

Dark Night of the Soul by St. John of the Cross

Saints Are Not Sad by Frank Sheed

Prayer Primer by Fr. Thomas Dubay, S.M.

PRAY FOR

_____

_____

_____

_____

_____

_____

_____

_____

_____

_____

_____

_____

_____

_____

_____

PRAY FOR

_____

_____

_____

_____

_____

_____

_____

_____

_____

_____

_____

_____

_____

_____

_____

_____

_____

PRAYER NOTES

PRAYER NOTES

PRAYER NOTES